Essential
Rhodes

by

GERRY CRAWSHAW

Gerry Crawshaw is a highly experienced
travel writer. He contributes to numerous
magazines and journals, and has also
written guides to a variety of countries,
including Essential Travel Guides to the
Algarve and Southern Portugal, Corfu,
Switzerland and Turkey.

AA

Produced by AA Publishing

Written by Gerry Crawshaw
Peace and Quiet section
by Paul Sterry
Series Adviser: Ingrid Morgan
Series Controller: Nia Williams
Copy Editor: Audrey Horne

Edited, designed and produced by
AA Publishing. Maps ©
The Automobile Association 1992

Distributed in the United Kingdom
by AA Publishing, Fanum House,
Basingstoke, Hampshire, RG21 2EA.

The contents of this publication are
believed correct at the time of
printing. Nevertheless, the
publishers cannot accept
responsibility for errors or
omissions, nor for changes in details
given. We have tried to ensure
accuracy in this guide, but things do
change and we would be grateful if
readers could advise us of any
inaccuracies they may encounter.

A CIP catalogue record for this book
is available from the British Library.

ISBN 0 7495 0316 5

Published by The Automobile
Association

Typesetting: Microset Graphics Ltd,
Basingstoke
Colour separation: BTB Colour Repro,
Whitchurch, Hampshire
Printed in Italy by Printers SRL,
Trento

*Front cover picture: Town harbour
and windmills*

Author's Acknowledgements
The author is indebted to Hogg
Robinson Travel for permission to
make use of regularly updated
information on holiday resorts and
hotels in Rhodes.

This book employs a
simple rating system to
help choose which
places to visit:

◆◆◆   do not miss

◆◆   see if you can

◆   worth seeing if
      you have time

INTRODUCTION

The Greek island of Rhodes – Rhódos or Rodas,
as it is known locally – has practically
everything anyone could possibly expect from
a holiday island . . . delightful beaches nestling
in craggy bays or stretching beyond eyesight;
sun-bleached villages rising up the side of hills
and mountains; and the spirit of an island
steeped in centuries of history and mythology.
When Helios, the Sun God, blessed it with light
and warmth and favoured it with a delightful
climate and lush vegetation, he may not have
thought that Rhodes would one day become the
most visited of the Dodecanese islands. And
though resorts have mushroomed along the
coastline offering varied facilities and
entertainment to satisfy most visitors' needs, the
people of Rhodes are still likely to greet you
with genuine warmth and hospitality and to take
great pride in sharing with you their jewel in
the sea.

The largest of the Dodecanese islands, Rhodes
is in the Aegean Sea, on the southeastern edge
of the Dodecanese, facing Turkey 10 miles

Statues of a stag and a doe stand guard over the harbour at Rhodes

(16km) away. Smaller than Crete but larger than Corfu, it is approximately diamond shaped, being about 40 miles (65km) long and 25 miles (40km) wide, and enjoys a mild climate and long, sun-drenched summer days.

Thanks to its situation at the crossroads of three continents, the island has known many masters. Romans, Crusaders, Arabs, Turks and Italians have all left their mark, and today's visitors can marvel at the ruins of ancient temples, admire elaborate mosques, wander narrow streets flanked by medieval inns, soak up the centuries-old atmosphere of the island's enchanting towns and villages, or venture inland to enjoy the rugged, olive-clad hillsides sheltering scented pine forests.

Rhodes is so different from most Greek isles that even Greeks tend to describe it as 'foreign'. Side by side you will find sophistication and simple Greek life, luxury hotels and little tavernas, smart entertainment and simple pleasures.

There are good beaches all around the coast, some with watersports, bars, smart restaurants

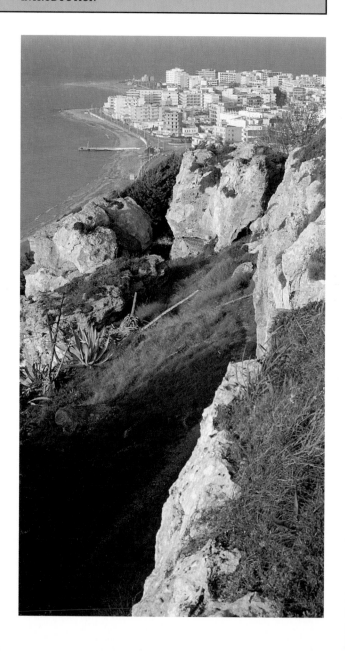

Named after an English admiral, Monte Smith was once a suburb of ancient Rhodes, until the town shrank and nature reclaimed the hill

and entertainment; others simple and almost deserted. And though midsummer temperatures can reach 30°C (85°F) and above, west winds soften the heat on many beaches.

Rhodes Town, the island's capital, is a remarkable and attractive blend of a lively harbour, a walled, fortified medieval town and a cosmopolitan, modern town.

Most visitors to the east coast of Rhodes understandably opt for Líndhos, built on the ruins of an ancient Doric town of the same name. Despite being overrun by tourists in the high season, and commercialised to a degree many people consider unacceptable, there can be no denying that it is still a delightful, magical place . . . a little town of whitewashed houses built on the sides of a steep, rocky hill, crowned by an awe-inspiring castle built by the Knights of St John of Jerusalem.

There are many other delights on the east coast of Rhodes in addition to Líndhos. The former spa resort of Thermai Kallithéa is built round a colourful, pine-covered bay; Falirakion is a lively, cosmopolitan holiday resort with an excellent beach; Afándou is an ancient village with a golf course and an interesting church; and Tsambika has a lovely, sandy shoreline as well as a mountain topped with a monastery dedicated to the Virgin Mary. The village of Arkhángelos is noteworthy for its traditional architecture, ceramics and carpet workshops, while Kharákion, a former fishing village that is now a fast-developing holiday resort, lies on a lovely stretch of coast that contains the impressive ruins of Feraklos castle.

Popular holiday resorts, important archaeological sites and picturesque villages are to be found on the northwest coast of the island too, beginning with Rhodes Town itself and embracing the resorts of Triánda, on the doorstep of the impressive ancient city of Ialyssos, with its magnificent acropolis; the blossoming resort of Kremastí; and, slightly inland, the unusual Valley of the Petaloudhes (Butterflies), where from June to early September many thousands of butterflies (or, more correctly, moths) take refuge.

Then there is ancient Kamiros, the island's third most important commercial city in ancient times; the delightful fishing village of Kamiros Skala; and fascinating Monólithos, built on the pine-covered slopes of Mount Atáviros, with a 15th-century castle on the cliffs.

Rhodes also has much to offer the visitor prepared to venture inland, with delightful, traditional villages little touched by tourism, and areas of great scenic beauty such as Profítis Ilías, with its panoramic sea views.

But there is more to Rhodes than well situated holiday resorts, historic sites and lovely landscapes. Modern hotels offer every comfort, and shopping is a pleasure. There is plenty for the active visitor too, with tennis, watersports, lovely walks and a well-designed golf course – to say nothing of cycling, a popular form of transport here. As for restaurants, tavernas, bars and discothèques, these abound in the major coastal resorts, and in Rhodes Town itself, with a sufficiently wide choice to cater for most tastes and pockets. And Rhodes' geographical position also provides for some interesting visits to other nearby islands; excursions to Simi are particularly popular with those choosing Rhodes as a holiday base.

Some areas of Rhodes have been allowed to grow excessively and haphazardly in the pursuit of tourist dollars. However, the Greek authorities are now imposing much stricter controls on all the country's top holiday destinations, including Rhodes. In particular, the authorities are stressing the need for 'quality' in every aspect of tourism, not least the accommodation sector, and the Greek Parliament is introducing a star system for all Greek hotels as part of its campaign to raise standards generally.

The government also believes that tourism in Rhodes and other areas of Greece is still sufficiently cheap for prices to be raised a little, provided this is accompanied by an improvement in standards. For this reason the National Tourist Organisation of Greece is becoming tougher in its hotel inspections, and a closer watch on standards will be made possible by the planned re-establishment of the Tourist Police – moves which should all help maintain Rhodes' reputation as one of the best holiday destinations in Europe for visitors of all ages.

BACKGROUND

According to mythology, Rhodes was singled out for favour by the sun god Helios who, having been overlooked when Zeus distributed the lands of the world among the gods, discovered the island and made it his own, together with the beautiful nymph Rhodos, daughter of the sea god Poseidon, whom he took for his wife.

Ancient Rhodes grew rich on sea trade and, according to legend, the favour of the sun god

Beginnings

The first human inhabitants of the island are thought to have been a rugged, primitive people from Asia Minor who possessed great skills in the arts. On the basis of discoveries made in a cave in southern Rhodes, experts believe they settled there as early as the Stone Age, though it is thought they were subsequently overrun by waves of invaders during the Bronze Age – Carians from Anatolia, Phoenicians from present-day Lebanon, and Minoans from Crete.

The most significant early invaders, however, were the Achaeans from the Peloponnese who,

One of the Seven Wonders of the World, the Colossus of Rhodes stood over 100 feet (30m) high

by 1500BC, had colonised the island. These were, in turn, replaced by Dorians who swept through Greece about 1100BC. On Rhodes they built shrines for moon worship at Ialyssos, Líndhos and Kamiros, and also united with the island of Kos and the cities of Knidos and Halicarnassus in Asia Minor to form a federal league, the Dorian hexapolis.

For centuries the inhabitants of Rhodes, especially the men of Líndhos, were great sailors. Their trading ventures took them to Asia, Greece and as far as the western Mediterranean. Rhodian colonies were founded in the west – in Sicily, Spain and France.

Classical Period

In 491BC Rhodes fought off the first attempt by Persian forces to take the island. Datis, who led the Persian attack, laid siege to Líndhos but withdrew his forces on learning that the goddess Athena had performed a miracle and supplied the water that the local population so desperately needed. The island was forced to become a Persian ally in the years that followed, however, and when Xerxes invaded the Greek mainland in 480BC, 40 of the ships which fought on the Persian side at Salamis were Rhodian. The Greek victory in this great sea battle saw Rhodes enter a period of subjugation to Athens, and at the end of the Persian wars the three cities on Rhodes (Ialyssos, Líndhos and Kamiros) became members of the 1st Athenian Confederacy (478/77BC). Then, towards the end of the 5th century BC, the Rhodians decided to found a new city on the northern tip of the island – a model, walled city designed by the leading town planner of the day and sited to satisfy defence and trade needs, with five new harbours.

The new city soon became the major trading power in the eastern Mediterranean and one of the great cultural centres of the Hellenistic and Roman worlds. As it increased in importance, the three older cities suffered a gradual decline.

The city of Rhodes' pre-eminence lasted for several centuries. In the third century BC, for example, its population is estimated to have been between 60,000 and 80,000, two or three times larger than that of today. And the contribution of the island to the arts, trade and law of the time was significant.

In the troubled period that followed the death of Alexander the Great, however, Rhodes was attacked in 305/304BC by a huge force led by Demetrios (son of one of Alexander's generals and himself a brilliant commander), using modern technical equipment in the attempt. When Demetrios came to Rhodes he was already known as 'The Besieger', a title gained following his success against a city in Cyprus. The siege of Rhodes, however – which lasted a year – failed to justify his reputation, with the city emerging intact largely thanks to its strong defence walls. The Rhodians sold the siege machines left behind by Demetrios and used the huge revenue from the sale to erect a tribute to their god Helios – the Colossus of Rhodes. The mighty statue was to collapse during an earthquake in 226BC.

In 164BC Rhodes entered into an ill-fated alliance with Rome which culminated in an attack by Cassius in 42BC. Cassius sacked the island, stripped it of many thousand works of art which he sent to Rome, confiscated public and private money, allowed the citizens to be butchered, and finally set fire to what was left.

Medieval Rhodes

Christianity took root in Rhodes during the 1st century AD, aided by St Paul, who visited the island on his way to Syria, about 20 years after the Crucifixion. But this did not lead to a period of peace or stability, and by the end of the 4th century AD, Rhodes had exchanged the rule of Rome for that of Byzantium. However this, too, did not lead to happier times. Indeed, in the ensuing centuries the island was attacked by numerous invaders . . . Goths in the 5th century, Arabs in the 7th and 9th centuries, and then Saracens, Venetians, Franks and Genoese. Rhodes' ties with western Europe were strengthened in 1097 with the appearance of the Crusaders on their way to the Holy Land. In 1191, King Richard the Lionheart of England and King Philip Augustus of France landed in Rhodes to recruit mercenaries. Byzantium was captured by the Crusaders 13 years later, and the tide of battle turned. By 1291 the Christian army was forced off the beaches at Acre, today part of Israel.

Knights of St John

Among the retreating soldiers were the Knights of the Order of St John of Jerusalem – or Knights Hospitallers as they are sometimes referred to in order to distinguish them from the Knights Templars, members of the Order of the Poor Knights of Christ.

The Knights of St John originated in the 11th century at the Hospital of St John in Jerusalem, a Benedictine hospital for pilgrims. The Order was founded to care for the poor and sick, train doctors, protect pilgrims, and make war on the infidel. Their first patron was St John the Almsgiver, a 6th-century Cypriot bishop, and in 1113 the Order and its possessions were taken under the protection of Pope Paschal II in gratitude for the services which the hospital had provided during the Crusades.

The Knights of St John took an active part in the Crusades but, following the fall of the last Christian stronghold in Palestine, they were driven out of Palestine not only by the forces of Saladin but through bitter rivalry with the powerful Knights Templars.

The Knights of St John emigrated to Cyprus in 1291, but in 1309 decided to transfer to Rhodes, believing this to be a better base. However, the Greek pirates who had taken over the island in 1248 refused to allow the Knights to settle there. Undeterred, they decided to buy it, and a bill of sale was drawn up and witnessed.

The Knights nevertheless had to fight for their rights, defeating – with the aid of the Genoans – the Turkish garrison placed on the island by the Byzantine emperor. Once settled on Rhodes, the Knights established a hospital, continued to improve the island's defences, and for two centuries succeeded in holding out against marauding Turkish corsairs, building up a powerful fleet of war galleys, and becoming in the process excellent seamen.

Members of the Order of St John came from all the European Catholic countries, and were divided into classes based on the degree of nobility of their origins and the services they offered as soldiers, nurses or clerics. The organisation was based on the country of origin, and they were divided into seven Tongues (ie languages) or national groups: Provence, Auvergne, France, Italy, Germany, England and Spain (which was later divided into Aragon and Castille, increasing the number of Tongues to eight). United by vows of obedience and chastity, they were divided into five groups: Military Knights, Conventual Chaplains, Serving Brothers, Magistral Knights and Knights of Grace.

It was the Military Knights who gave the Order its distinctive characteristics and from whom the Grand Masters were chosen. Before being admitted to the Order they were required to prove noble birth on both sides of their families for at least four generations, and so honourable was a career in this aristocratic foreign legion considered that it became the practice to put younger sons' names down at birth, with the promise of a large dowry.

As the Knights' wealth and power increased, the Turks launched a large-scale attack in 1479, but were driven back. The following year, however, Sultan Souleïmán I decided to launch another attack. His force of 70,000 men aboard 200 ships landed near Ialyssos on 24 June, and three months later laid siege to Rhodes with the sultan in command. In four and a half months Souleïmán lost 50,000 men trying to penetrate the fortified city, one attack resulting in the death of 9,000 Turks and half the Knights. The surviving Knights immediately set about rebuilding and improving the defences, and within a short time Rhodes became the strongest fortress in the west. But the Turks were undeterred, and 42 years later launched an even more massive attack. Although heavily outnumbered, the Knights put up a spirited defence, so much so that the Turks were on the verge of giving up, only to have second thoughts when a traitor revealed that victory was in their grasp. The invaders launched a final assault, and succeeded in breaching the massive walls. The Rhodian population called for a truce. As a result, after 145 days of siege the 180 surviving Knights, together with 4,000 Catholic Rhodians, were allowed to depart on 1 January 1523. They returned to Cyprus, and nine years later were given the sovereignty of Malta by the Emperor Charles V, after which they were generally known as the Knights of Malta. They remained in control of Malta until 1798 when they were deposed by Napoleon and took refuge in Russia. The Order was reconstituted in 1879 by the papacy as a charitable organisation for the care of the sick and wounded, the Order's emblem being a white Maltese cross on a black background.

Turkish and Italian Occupation

For nearly four centuries, until 1912, Rhodes remained a minor Turkish possession. Reminders of the Turks' occupation can be seen in the walled town, with its mosques and minarets, Turkish fountains and carvings and Turkish courtyards.

The Italians came to Rhodes in 1912, and occupied the island until 1943. Although the people at first regarded them as liberators from the hated Turkish rule, their time there was one of great hardship and oppression for the island – much more so than under the Turks – yet the Italians did leave behind them good roads, well-landscaped gardens, a number of public buildings and a great many private villas. During their occupation they also rebuilt the Palace of the Grand Masters (they regarded themselves as heirs of the Knights of St John) and undertook a considerable amount of restoration on classical sites.

Anáktoro ton Arkhónton has been in turn the Knights' headquarters, a Turkish prison and an Italian palace

Recent Times

After the fall of Mussolini's government in 1943, Rhodes was occupied by German troops until 1945 when Greek and British forces recaptured the island. Following a period of United Nations trusteeship, it was reunited with Greece in 1947, and is now the administrative capital for the islands which make up the Dodecanese – notably Astipálaia, Khálki, Kárpathos, Kásos, Tílos, Nísiros, Kálimnos, Léros, Pátmos, Rhodes, Simi, Kos, Psérimos and Lipsói.

The population of Rhodes today is about 67,000 with the biggest concentration in Rhodes Town. The enormous development of tourism has

transformed Rhodes' economy in recent years,
although part of the population is still engaged
in agriculture and stock-breeding. The
cultivable area of the island forms about 18 per
cent of the whole, the main products being
wine, oil, tobacco, garden produce, cereals and
other crops. Cattle raising is also important,
since 34 per cent of the terrain is pastureland.
The forests are also a source of revenue,
covering 37 per cent of the territory, and are
home to a type of deer known as *platoni* – a
rare animal that is one of Rhodes' emblems, and
a protected species.

DODECANESE

RHODES TOWN

Platia Ippokratous, Old Town

Rhodes Town is situated at the northern tip of the island, and is one of the busiest and liveliest resorts in the whole of Greece, attracting visitors from all over Europe. It is a captivating town. The powerful impression given by the great walls and dominant Palace of the Grand Masters (Anáktoro ton Arkhónton), is tempered by elegant minarets and colonnades and gardens lush with greenery and bright with bougainvillea and hibiscus. The town comprises two quite separate but complementary sections – the ancient, medieval walled city known as the Old Town; and the modern city known, not surprisingly, as the New Town. Both sections are well worth visiting.

The Old Town, with its impressive, 15th-century buildings, cobbled streets and alleys ornamented with arches and vaults, its impressive museums, countless shops, scores of atmospheric bars, tavernas and restaurants, and traditional coffee shops, is understandably the jewel in the crown. Here you will find such riches as the unique Street of the Knights, arguably the most splendid medieval street in the world, although heavily restored in recent years; the fascinating Museum of Rhodes (Arkheologikó Mousío), housed in a 15th-century building which originally served as the hospital of the Knights of St John; the Museum of Decorative Arts (Mousío tis Kosmikís Technís), with its interesting display of folk art; and the equally interesting Municipal Art Gallery (Astikí Pinakothíki), with its exhibition of modern art by Greek painters. Here, too, you will find the impressive Palace of the Grand Masters, built on the site of an ancient temple

RHODES TOWN

dedicated to Rhodes' patron deity, the sun god Helios, and now a museum; the Turkish baths, still in use; and numerous 16th-century mosques built by Souleïmán the Magnificent. Whereas the Old Town is a treasure-trove of towers, battlements, mosques and fine medieval buildings and streets, the New Town is where the beaches lie and where hotels, shops, restaurants, discothèques and even a casino are packed together to create a lively, cosmopolitan ambience. The New Town also contains much to interest the sightseer, including bustling Mandraki Harbour, where floating gin-palaces rub sterns with more traditional boats; the Neá Agorá (New Market), has an internal courtyard alive with stalls, a fish market, and shops, cafés and bars.

Other impressive buildings on or near the harbour are the Archbishop's Palace (Paláti Arkheiepiskopou), Church of the Annunciation (Eklissía Evangelismós), Town Hall (Dimarcheíon), and National Theatre (Ethnikó Théatro), while also of particular interest in the New Town are the Mosque (Tzamí) of Mourad Reïs, with its graceful minaret, and the Aquarium (Enydríon).

Rhodes Town has two beaches, both extremely crowded in the high season, and consisting mainly of coarse sand. That on the east side of town is sandier than that on the west, which has a busy main road running behind it. Children need to be supervised, since the sea bed shelves steeply.

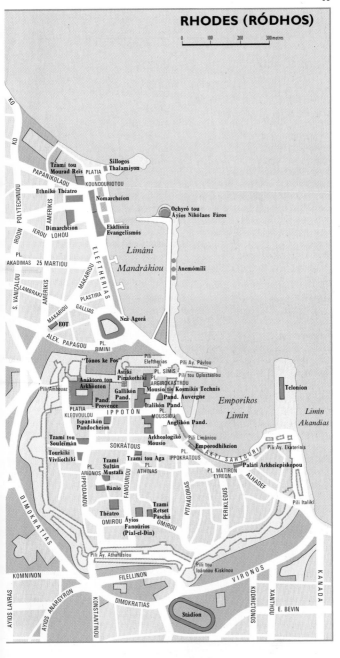

RHODES (RÓDHOS)

0   100   200   300 metres

KO

PAPANIKOLAOU
Tzamí tou
Mourad Reís
PLATIA
Síllogos
Thalamíyon
KOUNDOURIOTOU

IROON POLYTECHNIOU
Ethnikó Théatro
AMERIKIS
Nomarcheíon

IEROU LOHOU
Dimarcheíon
Ekklissía
Evangelismós
Ochyró tou
Áyios Nikólaos Fáros

PL. AKADIMAS   25 MARTIOU
Limáni
Mandrákiou
Anemómili

S. VANIZALOU
LAMBRAKI
AMERIKIS
MAKARIOU
ELEFTHERIAS
PLASTIRA
GALLIAS

MAKARIOU
EOT
Neà Agorá

ALEX. PAPAGOU
PL. RIMINI

"Tónos ke Fos"
Pili
Eleftherias
Pili Ay. Pávlou
Pili tou Oplostasíou
Astiki
Pinakothiki
PL. SÍMIS
PL.
ARGIROKASTROU
Anáktoro ton
Arkhónton
Gallikón
Pand.
Mousío tis Kosmikis Technís
Pand. Auvergne
Pili Ambouaz
Pand.
Provence
Italikón Pand.
Teloníon
PLATIA
KLEOVOULOU
Ispanikón
Pandocheíon
IPPOTÓN
PL.
MOUSSIOU
Anglikón Pand.
Emporikos
Limín
Limín
Akandías

Tzamí tou
Souleïmán
Arkheologikó
Mousio
Pili Limáníou
SOKRATOUS
Emporodhikeíon
PL.
Tourkiki
Vivliothiki
Tzamí tou Aga
IPPOKRATOUS
Pili Ay. Ekaterínis
AKTI SAHTOÚRI
PL.
APPODAMOU
Tzamí
Sultán
Mustafá
PL.
ATHINAS
PL. MATIRON
EYREON
Palátí Arkheiepiskopou
ALHADEF
FANOURIOU
Bánio
PITHAGORAS
PERIKLEOUS
Pili Italikí

DIMOKRATIAS
Théatro
OMIROU
Tzamí
Retset
Paschá
Áyios
Fanoúrios
(Pial-el-Din)
OMIROU

Pili Ay. Athanasíou
Pili tou
Ioánnou Kiskínou
VIRONOS

KOMNINON
FILELLINON
KODRICTONOS
XANTHOU
E. BEVIN
KANADA

AYIOS LAVRAS
AYIOS ANARGYRON
KONSTANTINOU
DIMOKRATIAS
Stádion

WHAT TO SEE

◆◆◆
ANÁKTORO TON ARKHÓNTON
(Palace of the Grand Masters)

Platia Kleovoulou, Old Town
Dominating the northeast sector
of the city's fortifications, this
imposing, turreted building –
now a museum – is a
reconstruction of a palace built
by Helion de Villeneuve on the
site of an ancient temple to the
sun god Helios. After serving as
the Knights' palace, it was
turned into a prison by the
Turks, who also used it for
stabling their horses. Following
centuries of neglect it was
destroyed by an ammunition
explosion in the palace vaults in
1856. The explosion – thought to
have been set off by lightning –
killed an estimated 800 people.
The palace was rebuilt, in
questionable taste, by the
Italians as a summer home for
Mussolini and Victor Emmanuel
III. Because of its intended use,
it was made even grander than
the original. The exterior you
see today is a reasonable
approximation of the
14th-century original, and was
completed by the Italians just
before the outbreak of World

Anáktoro ton Arkhónton's great door

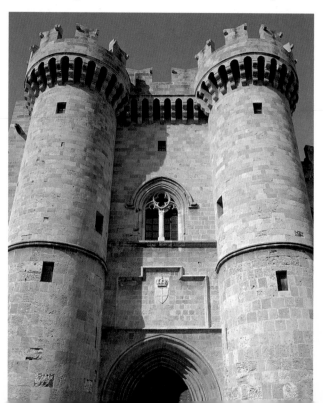

War II. Inside, they installed central heating, concealed lifts, translucent alabaster windows, Roman statuary and ancient mosaics. But the interior was scarcely completed when the Italian occupation came to an end.

The great door of the palace between the two round towers is one of the parts preserved from the original building. Beyond it is a large, covered area, with the entrance to the main building on the left, and straight ahead an interior courtyard surrounded by arches containing a variety of statues. A small chapel standing at the foot of the marble staircase contains some Roman and early Christian objects.

Inside, a marble staircase leads to rooms paved with mosaics and furnished with statues, Italian furniture, wall carpets and Chinese vases. Of the palace's 200 rooms – 14 of which are open to the public – the most impressive are the throne and ceremonial rooms.

The fine Roman and early Christian mosaics displayed throughout the palace are not part of the original furnishing, but were removed from the nearby island of Kos by the Italians. The most interesting is a 1st-century AD representation of the nine Muses covering the floor of an entire room. The long passages are furnished with numerous choir stalls.

Excellent views of the town and surroundings can be enjoyed from the palace windows and also from its garden.

Open: daily 08.30–15.00hrs. Closed Mondays.

◆◆◆
ARKHEOLOGIKÓ MOUSÍO
(Museum of Rhodes)
Platia Moussiou, Old Town

The most important antique objects discovered in Rhodes and the other islands making up the Dodecanese are displayed in the impressive medieval building that was once the Hospital of the Knights of St John of Jerusalem. Construction of the building began in 1440 when the Knights' original hospital became too small, and it was completed in 1489, in Gothic style. In common with most of the Street of the Knights (see page 25), the building was restored in the 1900s, and has been a museum since 1916.

With an arcaded courtyard and a wide flight of steps leading to a gallery which runs round three sides of the square, almost the whole of the building's east side is occupied by the **Infirmary Hall**, widely considered one of the most impressive medieval rooms in Europe. Nearly 100 yards (90m) long, it has a vaulted roof supported by arches springing from the seven pillars which divide the hall lengthwise. In this chamber there was room for 32 canopied beds for sick or wounded Knights, attended night and day by surgeons and orderlies, the care of the sick being the original reason for the Order's foundation.

At the south end of the hall a door leads into a room which served as the hospital refectory, and this in turn leads into three rooms which house the museum's collection of statuary. The rooms on the south side of the museum display finds from the excavations of cemeteries in the area of ancient Ialyssos – mostly vases from the 9th to 5th centuries BC. In the centre of the east side is the entrance to the infirmary, containing gravestones from the period of

Medieval coats of arms on display in the Arkheologikó Mousío

the Knights, and many coats of arms, while the refectory or dining room for hospital staff is used to display funerary stele (columns) from the Roman period. Of particular interest here is a beautifully executed and preserved funerary stele of two female figures – Timarista, on the right, and her daughter Krito – embracing in a final farewell.

Of the museum's many exhibits, however, one of the most impressive is the tall figure of the **Aphrodite of Rhodes**, otherwise known as the 'Marine Venus', having been found in the sea by fishermen early this century. It is on display in what is known as the **Room of the Small Aphrodite**. Aphrodite is represented kneeling, either before or after bathing, in a posture suggesting she is either

loosening or tying up her hair, and the artist has succeeded in showing off the female form to good advantage. Such statues adorned the houses of wealthy Rhodians around 100BC, and were also used as ornaments in public gardens. The Aphrodite of Rhodes is an example of ancient rococo which flourished at the end of the Hellenistic period in Rhodes – an art that sought to titillate the senses and capture a fleeting moment. The same room also contains a series of small statues, the most impressive of which is that of Asklepios (god of healing) with a snake twined round his staff. From here you come out on to a delightful gallery planted with flowers and shrubs which looks down on a small courtyard with a 6th-century mosaic pavement brought from Kárpathos. On the north side of the gallery are two rooms with more exhibits of considerable interest. One, labelled 'Hekataion', shows three female figures standing on the backs of lions. This was discovered on the acropolis (Monte Smith). Look out also for the fine, headless statue of a nymph with her foot on a rock, which dates from the 1st century BC.

The museum's courtyard displays a medley of exhibits: a marble crouching lion, some 2,000 years old; piles of cannon balls from the time of the Turkish invasion; catapult shot; and a mosaic, dating from 650BC, from Arkasa on the island of Kárpathos, between Rhodes and Crete.

Open: daily 09.00–15.00hrs. Closed Mondays.

◆
ASTIKÍ PINAKOTHÍKI
(Municipal Art Gallery)
Platía Símis, Old Town
A modern building in medieval style, this features exhibitions of modern art by Greek painters, and is located up a flight of stairs over the Ionian and Popular Bank. Of particular note are the works by Theophilos, an artist from the island of Mytilini (Lesbos), who specialised in the primitive style. An itinerant artist, Theophilos died in 1934. *Open:* daily 08.00–14.00hrs and also on Wednesdays 17.00–20.00hrs.

◆◆
AYIOS FANOÚRIOS
Old Town
The original Byzantine church and its frescos were taken over by the Turks who, at first, used the building as stables, destroying the lower wall paintings. Later it was converted into the Pial-el-Din Mosque, only for the Greeks to reclaim it and reconvert it to the Orthodox faith. The Italians restored the paintings towards the end of their occupation of Rhodes.

Byzantine frescos grace Ayios Fanoúrios's barrel vault

◆◆
BÁNIO (Bath House)
Old Town
The fantastic Turkish baths on Platia Arionos, in the southwest corner of the Old Town, is one of only a few public baths in Greece still in use. Constructed in 1765, the building was seriously damaged during World War II and subsequently rebuilt. The old marble floor remains, and the reconstruction was carried out sympathetically. Sexes are strictly segregated in the sauna.
Open: Monday–Friday 05.00–19.00hrs and slightly shorter hours on Wednesdays and Saturdays, when admission charges are cheaper. Closed Sundays.

◆
EMPORODHIKEÍON (Tribune of Commerce)
Platia Ippokratous, Old Town
Completed in 1507, the building was the court-house of the Knights. The first floor is reached by wide, external stone steps and supported by columns which form a ground level arcade. The doorway, which is decorated with carved coats of arms, is worthy of a close look.

◆◆
ENYDRÍON (Aquarium)
New Town
Located within a building bearing the grandiose name of Hydrobiological Institute, standing at the northern extremity of Rhodes Town, the Aquarium houses embalmed marine and other animals and large tanks full of fish and associated underwater vertebrates, and is said to be the only museum of its kind in Greece.
Open: daily 09.00–21.00hrs.

Welcoming smile at the Enydríon, Rhodes' unusual aquarium

ISURUS OXYRINCHUS
GRE: ΚΑΡΧΑΡΙΑΣ
ENG: MACKEREL SHARK
FRA: MAKO
GER: MAKOHAI

♦♦♦
IPPOTÓN (Street of the Knights)
Old Town

Leading due east from the Palace Square, the beautiful, if much restored, Street of the Knights is lined with inns which once housed the Knights of St John according to the language they spoke. Each of the Seven (later Eight) Tongues of the Order had its own residence, five of them located in the street.

The **Inn of France** (Gallikón Pandocheíon) is the best preserved example, with an elaborate façade bearing an off-centre doorway decorated with seven coats of arms and crocodile gargoyles. The coats of arms belong to the Order of St John and to the two Grand Masters who built the inn – d'Amboise and d'Aubusson. The date above the pointed arch of the main entrance, 1492, is the year work on the building began. Visitors are welcome to inspect the building, which is still used occasionally as a recital hall and for exhibitions. Next to it is the **Inn of Spain** (Ispanikón Pandocheíon), built in a style reflecting its Catalan influence. Near this once stood the Church of St John, the Knights' chief place of worship. It was blown up in the gunpowder explosion of 1856 in the Palace of the Grand Masters. A replica of questionable authenticity was built by the Italians at Mandraki Harbour in 1925.

The **Inn of Italy** (Italikón Pandocheíon) was restored during the period of the Italian occupation to resemble the original building. Over the sculpted doors is the emblem of Fabrizio del Caretto, a Grand Master who died in 1479, a year before the Turkish Sultan Souleïmán's assault.

The **Inn of Provence** (Pandocheíon Provence) was a later addition to the street, dating from the early 16th century. It has a less ornate façade than its counterparts. Nothing remains of the **Inn of Germany** except for a plane tree which marks the site where it once stood.

(The **Inn of England** (Anglikón Pandocheíon) is situated not in Ippotón itself, but on Platia Moussiou, across from the Archaeological Museum, and was built in 1483. It was destroyed in 1851 by an earthquake, rebuilt in 1919 by the Italians and further restored by the British after World War II, following severe damage from shelling. Of particular interest is a room displaying the works of a leading modern goldsmith. The **Inn of Auvergne** (Pandocheíon Auvergne) is also situated away from the Street of the Knights on Platia Símis. Today it houses the state offices.)

Halfway down the street is a shady garden visible beyond locked gates. Containing a lovely Turkish fountain, the garden has been the subject of recent restoration.

One of the oldest buildings in the street is the **French Chapel**, containing a niche for a statue of the Virgin and Child with Fleur-de-lis. Next door is the chaplain's residence, now housing the Italian vice-consulate.

transported from Rhodes during World War II. A poignant plaque on the wall of the Synagogue on nearby Odhos Dosiadou records that 2,000 Rhodian Jews still resident when German troops took over the island in July 1943 were assembled in this square before being transported to concentration camps, only 50 surviving. The square is also the location of the 15th-century **Archbishop's Palace**, a mish-mash of Gothic and Renaissance architecture. This housed the archbishop of the Greek Orthodox church prior to Souleïmán the Magnificent's invasion.

Three sea horses in the fountain, Platia Matiron Eyreon

Modern cruisers and medieval windmills, Limáni Mandrákiou

◆◆
JEWISH QUARTER
Old Town
The old Jewish quarter lies to the east of the Koskinou Gate (Píli Koskinou). Its most prominent feature is the drum-shaped **fountain** in Platia Matiron Eyreon (Square of the Martyrs), which is topped by three bronze sea horses and decorated with blue tiles, in turn decorated with shells and marine creatures. The square is dedicated to the Jews

◆◆◆
LIMÁNI MANDRÁKIOU
(Mandraki Harbour)
New Town

Guarded by two pillars supporting a bronze stag and doe, the harbour area is packed with strollers and sightseers who come here to enjoy the flavour and animation as well as the cafés and bars. This is where the Municipal Tourist Office (in Platia Rimini) and the Neá Agorá are located, and where the taxis and buses stop. The harbour also houses a yacht marina, the local fishing boat fleet, excursion boats, and the smaller inter-island ferries. Shops backing on to the Neá Agorá sell olives and nuts and duty-free drinks, while popular spots for sitting and watching the world go by are the cafés underneath the arches opposite the harbour. Other attractions for visitors are the trio of picturesque **windmills**, dating from the late 1400s, in which grain for the cargo ships was milled, and the 15th-century **fortress of St Nicholas** (Ochyró tou Ayios Nikolaos Fáros) which still guards the harbour, though no longer in use. It was built in 1464 with funds supplied by Philip the Good of Burgundy. In 1480, during the second of the Turkish sieges, the fort was greatly strengthened around the base and was later elaborated still more. Within its walls is a small church, dedicated to St Nicholas. At the northern end of the harbour the **Governor's House** (Nomarchéion), with its Venetian Gothic arches, is also popular with photographers. The name Mandraki, meaning sheepfold, reflects the commercial function of the port in earlier days.

Platoni *guarding the harbour entrance*

Mandraki Harbour is also reputedly the location of one of the most famous statues of all time, the **Colossus of Rhodes**. A tribute to the sun god Helios, the statue was massive – more than 100 feet (30m) tall, and was cast in bronze by the sculptor Chares of Lindos. The work took him 12 years. A masterpiece of technical and artistic achievement, it was considered one of the Seven Wonders of the Ancient World. But it stood for little more than 60 years before being felled by an earthquake in 226BC. Modern scholars cast doubt on the traditional theory that the statue straddled the harbour, with its massive feet on either side allowing ships to pass between its legs.

◆◆◆
MONTE SMITH
about 1 mile (2km) west of Rhodes Town

This hill was the site of the ancient Hellenistic town of Rhodes. It makes a pleasant walk from the town in the evenings. The hill, originally known as Ayios Stephanos, has been known as Monte Smith since the time of the Napoleonic Wars, when the English admiral, Sydney Smith, established an observation post here in 1802. The ancient town was about four to five times the size of that of the present day, and spread like an amphitheatre up towards Monte Smith. Italian architects identified the remains of a **temple of Athena Polias and Zeus Polias** on the northernmost point of the hill. The temple was one of the city's most important shrines. To the south is a collection of buildings that formed one of the centres of Rhodian intellectual and artistic life. The Italians also partially rebuilt a 3rd-century BC **Temple of Apollo**. It is thought that the original temple was destroyed by the same earthquake that destroyed the Colossus of Rhodes in about 226BC. Below the Temple of Apollo – which is still a landmark to ships at sea – is a heavily restored **stadium**. Only a few of the rows of seats in the centre of the curve are from the 2nd century BC. To the north of the entrance to the stadium is a small **theatre**, also from the same period, and also partly restored. Its size indicates it was not the main theatre of the ancient city but was one used for musical and other events in honour of Apollo. To the southwest of the stadium are **tombs** and remains of the city's outer walls.

Monte Smith offers excellent views over the whole northwest coast. The panorama is particularly delightful at dusk, when the lovely sunsets for which Rhodes is renowned can be enjoyed to the full.

You can get to Monte Smith on the No 5 bus which leaves from the station near the Neá Agorá (New Market). The journey takes about half an hour. A taxi ride to the site is not expensive.

◆◆
MOUSÍO TIS KOSMIKÍS TECHNÍS
(Museum of Decorative Arts)
Platia Argirokastrou, Old Town
This folk-art museum contains local pottery, carpets, costumes and other domestic items. It is housed in what is thought to have been an arsenal. Of particular note is a reconstruction of a house interior. Featured are a loom and spinning wheel, a cradle and a woven baby-carrier. The fireplace has a cooking shelf set into it and on this are earthenware pitchers and other utensils. From the ceiling hangs a rush carrier to enable cheese to be kept well above floor level. Also of special interest is a glass case containing an impressive collection of plates and jugs from Nicaea (modern Iznik in Turkey), in the Rhodian style.
Open: 09.00–15.00hrs. Closed Mondays.

Adjoining the museum is the **Armeria Palace**, the earliest

Temple of Apollo, Monte Smith

Infirmary of the Knights. Now occupied by the Institute of History and Archaeology, its upper gallery has an intriguing relief carving of an hourglass.

◆◆
MUNICIPAL GARDENS
New Town
Located beneath the Palace of the Grand Masters, the gardens are the scene of *son et lumière* performances ('Tónos ke Fos' in Greek) each evening in the summer, and are a pleasant spot for an evening stroll or as an escape from the heat of the midday sun.

The audio-visual interpretations of the rise and fall of the Crusaders' town begin at 20.15hrs and last approximately one hour. An English language version is usually performed every night, except Sunday, with Swedish, German, French and Greek versions on alternative evenings, but it is wise to check schedules with the Tourist Office, since they can change.

◆◆
NEÁ AGORÁ (New Market)
New Town
This Turkish-style building faces Mandraki Harbour and encloses a large area crammed with fruit and vegetable stalls, fast food cafeterias, souvenir shops and,

to one side of the tree-shaded internal courtyard, the raised rotunda building of the Fish Market. The shops which occupy the arcaded area facing the harbour are, in the main, cafés and cake shops, while liquor, grocery and gift shops, as well as a number of small supermarkets, can be found on the market's external periphery. Entry to the inner courtyard is through various alleyways that pierce the façade of the

Taking a close look at the fishy business in the Neá Agorá

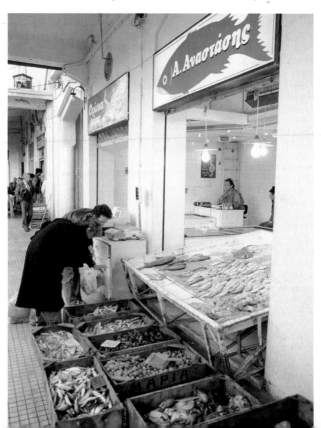

building. Any one of the cafés or restaurants in the area is a good spot to take in the sights, sounds and smells of the bustling market scene.

RODHINÍ PARK
about 2 miles (3km) east of Rhodes Town
This forested park, landscaped by the Italians, is a delightful, shady spot with rose gardens, lakes with rustic bridges, a mass of oleander bushes, flowers, cypresses and maples. It is also the site of a 3rd-century BC necropolis, or cemetery, containing among other finds a tomb, carved in the rock, and decorated with half-columns in the Doric style. Traditionally known as the **Tomb of Ptolemy**, it dates from the Hellenistic period and was restored by the Italians in 1924. Ptolemy was the general of Alexander the Great who conquered Egypt. The park is also thought to have been the site of a School of Rhetoric, founded in the 4th century BC, where many famous figures in Greek and Roman history, including Julius Caesar, studied.

In the summer months musical performances of bouzouki and international music are a regular feature, and the park also contains an enclosure with Rhodian deer. There is also a pleasant garden restaurant with a nightclub. The park was once the scene of an annual Wine Festival, held throughout the summer, but this has now been discontinued.

SON ET LUMIÈRE see **Municipal Gardens** page 29

TURKISH QUARTER
Old Town
The Turkish influence can be seen in the numerous minarets and arched windows in the part of the Old Town the Turks moved into after their successful conquest of Rhodes in 1522. The Christians resident there at the time were given until sunset to leave the island, and their churches were speedily converted into mosques by the addition of minarets. Latticed wood balconies characterise the narrow streets.

Until 1523 the Turkish quarter was known as the traders' quarter or Greek quarter, and is once again inhabited by Greeks. Near the **Mosque of Souleïmán** (see page 32) is the **Turkish Library** (Tourkikí Vivliothíki), containing valuable Turkish, Arab and Persian manuscripts. Of particular interest to the visitor are two beautifully decorated Korans, one dated 1412 and the other 1540. The library is housed in the rooms of the **Medresse Mosque** which was once a Greek church (dedicated to St George), and its attractive courtyard is decorated with pretty pebble mosaics. The **Mosque of the Aga** (Tzamí tou Aga), or Turkish commander, is located half way down Odhos Sokrátous and is unusual in that it is built on wooden, stilt-like legs. The **Retjep Pasha Mosque** (Tzamí Retset Paschá), on Odhos Omirou, was once the most beautiful mosque in Rhodes. Built in 1588 of material from several churches, it is now sadly abandoned.

◆◆
TZAMÍ TOU MOURAD REÏS
(Mosque of Mourad Reîs)
New Town

Located next to the National Theatre, at Mandraki Harbour, the shimmering white minaret of this mosque is arguably the most elegant on the island. It is approached through a cemetery leading to a shady yard paved in black and white. The mosque is to the left, and the tomb of Mourad Reïs lies within a small circular building on the right. Mourad Reïs was one of Souleïmán's admirals and was killed during the final assault on Rhodes in 1521–22.

The cemetery, built in 1523, is planted with a multitude of eucalyptus trees and crowded with Turkish headstones – an evocative place, away from the tourist bustle.

◆◆
TZAMÍ TOU SOULEÏMÁN
(Mosque of Souleïmán)
Odhos Sokrátous, Old Town

Erected by Souleïmán the Magnificent to show his gratitude for the conquest of the Knights in 1522, this is the largest mosque in Rhodes and the only one still used for worship. Its present-day appearance dates from 1808. The portal is thought to be from a church which once stood on the site. Inside, the mosque is spacious, quiet and pleasing, unlike most of the other mosques on the island, which are in a sorry state of neglect. It contains a stone minaret, red plaster walls and a Byzantine pulpit. The mosque is unfortunately not open to visitors.

◆◆
WALLS, GATES AND MOATS

The medieval military walls, towers and gates of the old quarter of Rhodes Town were constructed by the Knights, who also excavated the ditches. They were built, in part, on Byzantine foundations. After 1464 the fortress was divided into eight sectors or bulwarks which were allocated, for defence purposes, to the eight Tongues. After repulsing the Turkish siege of 1480, Italian engineers were commissioned to assist the then Grand Master, Pierre d'Aubusson, to strengthen the fortifications which, in places, resulted in wall thicknesses up to 40 feet (12m). The number of gates was reduced and the moat widened to some 65 feet (20m). In the 15th century the existing walls were reconstructed and strengthened by the Knights to improve defences against the Turks.

Of the gates (*píli*) in the walls the most most impressive are:
Amboise Gate (Píli Ambouaz). One of the grandest of them all, it leads, via a triple-arched bridge, over the outer moat and through the main part of the gate, bedded in the enormous walls.
Liberty Gate (Píli Eleftherias). A narrow gap busy with tourists and traffic, it leads to Platia Símis, containing a 3rd-century BC temple of Aphrodite. Constructed as recently as 1924, the gate was renamed in 1947 on the reunification of the Dodecanese islands with Greece.

The Esplanade roadway skirts the commercial harbour and is

Píli Eleftherias commemorates freedom

dominated by massive walls which are pierced by three gates – Arsenal (Píli tou Oplostasíou), Marine (Píli Limániou) and St Catherine's (Píli Ayia Ekaterínis). Particularly worthy of inspection is the bas-relief over the Marine Gate. The battlements run from the Customs Hall Quay (Teloníon) along the west side of the Acandia Harbour to the Gate of Italy, built in 1924. The Gate of St Athanasius (Píli Ayiou Athanasiou) was where Souleïmán the Magnificent breached the defences in 1522. Twice-weekly guided tours of the walls – on Mondays and Saturdays – start at the Palace of the Grand Masters, and last about one and a half hours. Check with the tourist information office for details.

Accommodation

Most hotels and self catering apartments in Rhodes Town are located in the New Town; visitors who want to stay in the more peaceful but mainly residential Old Quarter must look for pensions or private rooms (the tourist office will advise) although in high season these can be difficult to find.

Acandia Hotel, 61 Iroon Polytechniou (tel: 22251). A pleasant veranda where you can enjoy drinks or snacks is one of the features here. The 82 bedrooms all have private bath, balcony, telephone and radio. Grade B.

Athina Hotel, 27 Odhos G Leon (tel: 22634). Situated in a central position close to the beach and all the town's amenities and nightlife, with lounge, bar, lifts, large swimming-pool and solarium, and a breakfast room/restaurant. Grade B.

Belvedere, PO Box 144, Rhodes (tel: 24471). Only a short walk from the centre of Rhodes Town, this 165-room hotel overlooks a stretch of shingle and rocky beach, reached by subway. A modern, family-owned establishment on three floors, its facilities include a large, seawater pool with children's section, attractively-furnished sun terraces, and a restaurant serving both Greek and international dishes. Grade A.

Blue Sky Hotel, Platia Psaropoulas (tel: 24091). Right on the seafront, about five minutes' walk from the town centre. All 182 bedrooms have central heating, telephone, three-channel music, private bathroom and balcony. Many have splendid sea views. Amenities include shops, a hairdresser's and a nightclub featuring live music and Greek folklore shows. Because of its location on the main road and near a busy roundabout, the Blue Sky is not the best choice for those with small children. Other disadvantages include three-sided lifts and indecipherable depth markings in the pool. Grade A.

Chevalier's Palace, 3 Odhos G Griva (tel: 21360). This comfortable hotel is well situated just off the centre of the New Town, and close to the Grand Hotel Astir Palace. It is also well positioned for the town beaches, shops, harbour and the Old Town. Facilities include a restaurant, snack bar, night club, sauna, solarium, beauty parlour, heated seawater swimming-pool, mini-golf, tennis and badminton courts. Grade A.

Grand Hotel Astir Palace, 1 Odhos Akti Miaouli (tel: 26284). This long-established hotel is officially rated deluxe, though now in need of some refurbishment. Conveniently located within easy walking distance of the centre of Rhodes Town, it stands in its own grounds just across the road from the beach, where windsurfing and pedaloes are available. The hotel also has two outdoor seawater pools. For evening entertainment there is an international casino – the only one on the island – and a nightclub – 'Isabella'. Sports facilities include a floodlit tennis court and a games room with table tennis and electronic games. Children have their own swimming-pool. Deluxe.

Hotel Helena, 72 Odhos G Griva (tel: 22681). Within a ten-minute walk of the centre of Rhodes Town, the Helena is a clean, highly recommended family-owned hotel offering excellent value for money. It has a small but clean seawater pool, good sun terrace, and an attractive breakfast room opening on to the pool terrace. Warning notices indicate that three-sided lifts are operated. Grade C.

Ibiscus Hotel, PO Box 90 – 17 Odhos Nisirou (tel: 24221). A friendly, modern hotel located about ten minutes' walk from the beach and about a mile (1.5km) from the centre of town, the Ibiscus offers a terrace, lounge bar, two additional lounges, dining room, television room, card tables, and a popular steak house. Furniture is comfortable but somewhat basic. Grade A.

Lomeniz Hotel, Odhos CI Peper – Constadini (tel: 34649). This is a highly recommended, recent, 210-room hotel, located in a semi-residential area about a mile and a half (2.5km) from the centre of town but opposite a pleasant stretch of sandy beach. Facilities offered range from a swimming-pool – rather small considering the hotel's size – bar, taverna, garden, and facilities for table tennis and billiards. A minus point is that the marble floors can be very slippery. Grade B.

Marie Hotel, 7 Odhos Kos (tel: 30577). With a heated swimming-pool and sauna, the Marie claims to offer A-grade facilities at C-grade prices. Its 125 rooms all have balconies, bathrooms, telephones and music channels, and the hotel is situated opposite the town's park, about 100 metres/yards from the beach. Apart from the swimming-pool and sauna, other amenities include a bar, television lounge, pub and cafeteria. Grade C.

Mediterranean Hotel, 35-7 Odhos Kos (tel: 24661). This is an elegant medium-sized hotel enjoying a good location on the seafront opposite a busy stretch of shingle beach, and about ten minutes' walk from the bars, shops, restaurants and nightlife of the town centre. There is an attractively decorated lounge area, several bars, a large dining room, and an open-air patio with pleasant views. Grade A.

Park Hotel, 12 Odhos Riga Ferreou (tel: 24611). In a quiet, residential quarter of Rhodes Town yet only a few minutes' walk from the beach, the Park offers a restaurant, bar, verandas, gardens, and a large swimming pool. Grade A.

Hotel Spartalis, 2 Odhos N Plastira (tel: 24371). Just a couple of minutes' walk from Mandraki Harbour and ten minutes' walk from the beach, the Spartalis provides a good base from which to explore the town and take day trips to other islands. The rooms, which have been renovated, are of a good size and half have balconies overlooking the harbour. There is no entertainment provided in this hotel, but all the facilities of the town are within walking distance. The hotel is comfortable and the management efficient and friendly. Grade B.

Stella Guest House, 58 Odhos Dilveraki (tel: 24935). Charming and friendly, this small guest house is run by resident proprietors. Situated in the centre of the modern quarter of Rhodes Town, it is a few minutes' stroll from the nearest stretch of beach, and is a good choice for those on a tight budget. Grade B.

Restaurants

Rhodes Town offers an enormous choice of restaurants, tavernas, self-service cafeterias, take-away establishments, pastry shops, bars and cafés. Restaurants specialising in pizzas and spaghetti are to be found everywhere, and are relatively inexpensive.

Recommendations

Kon-Tiki (tel: 22477). An upmarket floating restaurant

located by the harbour jetty, the Kon-Tiki is popular with those looking for an unusual setting, although it is not cheap.

Casa Castella, 35 Odhos Aristotelous in the Old Town (tel: 28803). Not cheap, but wonderfully atmospheric, with the advantage of a delightful walled garden for al fresco eating (evening reservations recommended). Located in a house built in 1480, during the time of the Knights of St John, it has been a restaurant for 16 years, offering a good range of fish and steak dishes, with additional specialities such as *trahanas*, a traditional village soup. Brothers George and Nick Tsimetas are the gracious and talented hosts.

Both **Alexis** and **Fotis**, in Odhos Sokrátous, in the Old Town, are renowned for their excellent, if pricey, fish dishes, while **Melas**, near the Palace of the Grand Masters, has a reputation for good Greek cuisine, as does the moderately priced **Myconos**, in Odhos Papanikolaou in the New Town.

Other New Town recommendations include **Dania**, near the TUI office, which offers a cold Danish buffet every Sunday evening; **La Maison Fleurie**, Odhos Riga Ferreou, which specialises in French cuisine; and the fish restaurant **Sierra del Paella**, near the Aquarium.

If you enjoy the bustle and colour of markets, **Mamma Maria**, in the New Market, is simple and unsophisticated but serves delicious grilled chicken, meat and fish dishes at pavement tables.

Self-service/Fast Food
For those on a budget or looking for an inexpensive meal, the numerous self-service restaurants and cafeterias are a good bet. Particularly recommended are the **Yellow Spot**, Odhos G Griva; **Sally Brown's**, Odhos 25 Martiou; and **Chevalier's Corner**, attached to the Chevalier's Palace Hotel. Of the numerous pizzerias in town, **La Pizzagio**, at the corner of Platia Ayios Nikólaos, is particularly good.

Coffee Shops, Bars, Pubs
There are atmospheric coffee shops throughout Rhodes Town, most of them frequented by locals, who linger over their pastries, small cups of sweet coffee and glasses of water, sometimes playing backgammon. Recommended coffee shops include **Trianon**, in Platia Akadimas; **Rendez-vous**, Iroon Polytechniou; and **Etanh**, in Odhos Ammokhostou. Bars and pubs that are also popular with locals as well as visitors include **Belle Nuit**, Odhos Orfeos; and the **White Rock Pub** and the **Kahlua Cocktail Bar**, both in Odhos Othonos-Amalias. **Vivere** is a stylish piano bar off the lower end of Odhos Sokrátous in the Old Town.

Nightlife and Entertainment
Among the best discothèques and nightclubs are **Le Palais**, in Odhos 25 Martiou, next to the main Post Office, which features an atmospheric piano bar, discothèque and also a restaurant; **Play Boy**, Leoforos Ialyssou; **Obsession**, in the Panagos shopping centre at Monte Smith; and **Hiway**, in

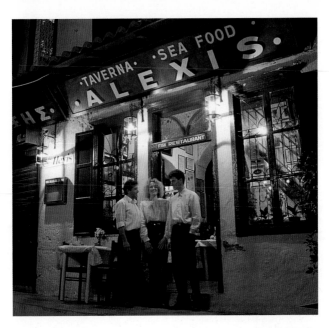

Alexis, a big name in the Old Town

Leoforos Ialyssou.
Greek folk dancing can be enjoyed at numerous establishments, including the restaurant **Don Kichotis**, at 24 Odhos Orfeos, in the Old Town. Other places specialising in bouzouki or folk music include **Café Chantant**, 22 Odhos Aristotelous, Old Town; **Melody**, 12 Odhos Riga Ferreou; **Rodos By Night**, opposite the Hotel Miramare' **New York**, 105 Leoforos Ialyssou; **Zorbas**, 4 Iroon Polytechniou; and the **Olympia** restaurant/coffee bar near the main Post Office. Authentic Greek dance and folk song performances are given every evening except Saturday from May to October at the **Old Town Theatre**, in the Old Town, (tel: 20157/29085).

Shopping
Anyone who likes shopping and window-browsing will enjoy Rhodes. There are shops, boutiques and mini-markets throughout the island, although most shoppers understandably make a bee-line for Rhodes Town, which has more than 4,000 shops situated in the modern shopping districts of the New Town area, and in the cobbled streets of the medieval walled city. The two markets (Palia Agorá and Neá Agorá) offer a variety of goods and plenty of local colour.
For information on good buys and where to make them see the chapter **Shopping** pages 95-7.

LÍNDHOS

Just 35 miles (56km) down the east coast from Rhodes Town, Líndhos is the island's second most important tourist spot, popular both for day trips and as a place to stay.

Your first glimpse of Líndhos – a National Historic Landmark and one of the most beautiful sites in Greece – is captivating . . . a cluster of small, dazzlingly white houses nestling on a hillside overlooking a curving bay of sparkling blue water and golden sand, and crowned by a magnificent fortress. And despite the hordes of tourists who descend on Líndhos each summer, the village remains charming, with a delightful labyrinth of narrow little alleyways which at times pass below shady canopies of vines. Líndhos possesses the only natural harbour on the island, which is presumably why it developed into, and remained, the most important of Rhodes' three great ancient cities – and indeed, one of the most important commercial cities of antiquity. It first appeared in history about the time of the Dorians, although there is evidence there was a Minoan settlement here prior to this period. Because the land surrounding Líndhos is not the most fertile on the island, its inhabitants turned towards the sea for their livelihood, becoming traders and fishermen, and Lindhian sailors explored and colonised as far away as Italy, France and Spain. As you look down on this little village and the bay, or up at the imposing acropolis, bear in mind that this was once a city famous for its commerce, its riches, its temples and its seamen, with a population at one time of 17,000, compared with today's 700 inhabitants.

St Paul visited Líndhos, landing, it is believed, at the little bay below the southern slopes of the acropolis. Then, in the Byzantine period, the acropolis was fortified, first by the Byzantines and then by the Knights of St John, during whose time on the island the fortresses of Líndhos, Feraklos and Ialyssos were the strongest outside Rhodes Town. Líndhos was excavated by Danish archaeologists early this century, while restoration work on the buildings in the acropolis was undertaken by the Italians. The village at the foot of the acropolis lies on the site of the ancient city, which seems to have been abandoned between the 6th and 10th centuries AD when the inhabitants went to live on the acropolis. It began to be re-inhabited in the 11th century and subsequently knew times of great fortune.

Today Líndhos enjoys a different kind of prosperity, as a holiday mecca. The sandy beach fringing the main bay is popular with youngsters and families, being gently shelving into the sea and offering safe bathing. It is ideal for learning to windsurf or waterski, and for those who simply wish to laze around and sunbathe the surrounding scenery is magnificent. A small, rocky outcrop separates the main bay from Pallas Beach, which is smaller but also sandy. Shops, tavernas and bars cluster

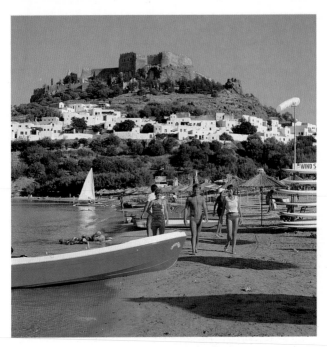

Fun and heritage combine in the spectacular beauty of Líndhos

around the main square and in the narrow alleyways and tiny, cobbled streets. Because Líndhos is the only community in Greece to be declared an official archaeological site, permission must be sought to make any repairs, changes, improvements or even to paint window shutters of its buildings. Notwithstanding the restrictions, former fishermen's houses have been converted into souvenir shops, bars or apartments, although, thankfully, the traditional feel of Líndhos persists. If only it did not attract quite so many visitors . . .

WHAT TO SEE

◆◆◆
ACROPOLIS

For a superb view of the village, the beach and the tiny harbour of St Paul, you will need to climb the uneven steps to the magnificent acropolis and hill-top fortress built in the Middle Ages by the Knights of St John. From here you can gaze down on the beach, crowded with sun-worshippers, and the bay alive with windsurfers and waterskiers. The walk up to the acropolis from the main square is steep, long and precipitous, which is why the most favoured means of transport is by donkey. But whether travelling on foot or

LÍNDHOS ACROPOLIS

by donkey, it is worth stopping to look at an unusual **rock carving** *en route*; thought to have been part of the base for a statue of a priest of Poseidon called Aghesandros, it represents the almost life-size stern of a Hellenistic ship complete with poop and steering paddles. The inscription tells us it was the work of the sculptor Pythokritos at the beginning of the 2nd century BC. Other rocks along the route are used by local women to display their crochet work and woven goods.

The final stage of the ascent is up a flight of steps leading through the main doorway into a vaulted hall above which, in medieval times, was the governor's palace. The gateway and hall were built by the Knights, and the hall is used for an informal display of Classical and Hellenistic pieces. Once through the hall you emerge into a paved yard. Turn left through a medieval, barrel-vaulted chamber and you come out into the lowest of the four terraces which, one above the other, mount to the temple. On this level the outer walls are on your left and some open storehouses on your right. There are also traces of a Doric and Corinthian temple at this level. Possibly dating from Roman times, it is popularly known as the **Whispering Temple**.

On the next level, reached by a short stairway, is a Doric stoa of the **Temple of Athena Lindia**, stretching some 100 yards (90m) on either side as you face it. The portico, or arcade, originally had 42 columns, of which 20 are now standing. The eight central columns of the façade stand in front of a monumental staircase leading to the propylaea (entrance). The small but elegant temple is thought to have been rebuilt after a fire in 345BC. It stands at the edge of a cliff which drops nearly 400 feet (120m) to the sea below, and was built in the Doric style, but with columns only at the front and rear, unlike most temples of the period.

A temple containing a statue of Athena is known to have existed here in the 10th century BC. By the middle of the 6th century BC an elaborate stone temple was erected by the then tyrant, Kleoboulus, but this building was later destroyed and the statue with it. In 348BC the Lindhians themselves built a temple and put into it a new statue of Athena, fashioned of wood, gold, marble and ivory, and wearing a wreath instead of a helmet. This house of the goddess Athena became one of the most important religious centres in Greece and the Mediterranean. It came to an end at the hands of the Emperor Theodosius of Byzantium, who removed to Constantinople many of its treasures, including the statue of the goddess.

The acropolis was used in Classical times both for ceremony and as a refuge for the people in times of war. The

The Acropolis looks down on the sea once sailed by the ancient ship shown in Pythokritos's carving

Knights of St John saw both advantages, though its real importance was as a military stronghold of the Order second only to Rhodes Town itself. The Grand Master, Foulques de Villaret, took sanctuary here when he was ousted from office in 1317.

After the Knights departed from Rhodes the Turks took over and in the middle of the 19th century they built houses on the acropolis and lodged a garrison there.

Open: daily 08.30–17.00hrs. Closed Mondays.

◆◆◆
LINDHIAN HOUSES

Líndhos is full of attractive, whitewashed houses, many dating from the 17th century and some built in Gothic style with Byzantine or oriental decoration. The oldest house is inscribed with the date 1599. Many of the houses are topped with small rooms to enable the owners to have a view of their ships in the harbour, and are known as the Houses of the Captains. Some have been restored and their interiors preserved as folk museums. The tourist information office in the main square will give further information on which houses are open to visitors.

Lindhian houses are solidly built, embellished with decorations of Byzantine doves, peacocks and flowers, or rope or chain patterns. Their interiors are characterised by high, wooden ceilings painted with floral designs, and their courtyards paved in decorative black and white *chochlaki* (pebble mosaic).

Some of the houses built since the 16th century are distinguished by a large, rectangular room known as 'the good house'. This contains a wide arch spanning nearly the full width of one wall, within which is built a long, low platform, reached by a flight of three steps. This platform was the family bed, generally ornamented with rugs or mats, with boldly embroidered pillows heaped in either corner. The wall above the bed platform is usually hung with Lindhian plates and embroidered cloths.

◆◆
ORMÍSKOS LÍNDHOS
(St Paul's Bay)

A small bay surrounded by bare rock, this is the spot where, it is claimed, a bolt of lightning and a clap of thunder caused the rock to split asunder creating a harbour that enabled a storm-tossed boat, bearing St Paul on one of his evangelising journeys, to reach safety. His arrival in AD51 is considered to be when Christianity reached the island and has given rise to the annual festival of St Paul here on 28 and 29 June.

◆◆
PANAYIA (Church of the Assumption of Our Lady)

Located near the main square, and dominating the centre of Líndhos, this delightful church has well preserved frescos by Gregory of Simi depicting well-known biblical scenes. They were painted in 1779 but restored in 1927. In one, St Francis is shown with the head of an ass. Above the main door is a delightful sequence showing people being weighed in the scales. Those found wanting are shown descending to hell, while the righteous are being elevated on little clouds. The 17th-century wooden sanctuary screen and bishop's throne are finely carved, and the floor is of black and white pebble mosaic, traditional to the Dodecanese islands. At the far end of the church is a burial chamber for priests of the church and certain citizens of the town. A number of 17th-century icons inside are well worth inspecting, notably the

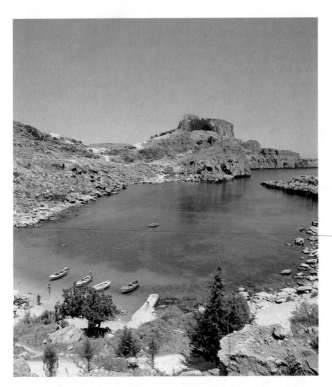

Ormískos Líndhos: calm waters

three immediately above the door. The centre one is of a Virgin and Child enclosed in a painted arc; on the left is a fine composition believed to be of an angel blessing a dying man in the presence of the prophet David with his harp and a company of angels. All the icons were the gifts of Lindhians to the memory of relatives buried in the room. The church is possibly older than the inscription of 1484–90, which could refer to a period of rebuilding by the Knights.

◆◆◆
THEATRE

The theatre of the ancient city is located on the western slope of the acropolis, facing the sea, and dates from the 4th century BC. It has 26 rows of seats. The amphitheatre is in fair condition – five of the gangways are clearly visible and four climb up through the lower slopes of seats to the higher ones. There is a decorated gangway dividing the two banks of seats. The lower bank is of 20 rows and at ground level there is the customary front row of stone chairs for the priests and other dignitaries. As you face the theatre, an excavated area marks the site of an ancient temple, possibly dedicated to Apollo. Later, a Byzantine chapel was built on the site, but this was demolished by the Italians at the beginning of World War II.

◆◆
TOMB OF KLEOBOULUS

Located near the northeast end of the harbour, looking down over the village, this is a giant, circular Hellenistic chamber made from square stone slabs. It dates possibly from the 5th or 4th century BC. It was later converted into a Christian church. Kleoboulus was a 6th-century tyrant leader of Líndhos, who ruled for 40 years and was one of the Seven Sages of the ancient world.

Accommodation

Because Líndhos is an official archaeological site and a conservation area, there are no hotels in the village itself, only small pensions and village rooms. These tend to be simple in the extreme, often verging on the basic, with few luxuries or modern furnishings. Many have what are described by tour operators as double bunker beds – a raised wooden platform on which there are either two separate mattresses or a double mattress. This is a layout typical of Líndhos and traditional Lindhian houses. The nearest hotels lie outside the village, at **Vliha Beach**, about 15 minutes' walk away. Atmospheric traditional Líndhos villas, studios and apartments

The secluded Lindos Bay Hotel

can be rented through Jenny May Holidays, 2–10 St Johns Road, London SW11 (tel (071) 228 0321).

Hotel Jota Beach (tel: 42205). This is a friendly, small, family-run hotel located next to a lovely stretch of beach. Although facilities are limited, guests are welcome to use those of the hotels Lindos Bay – about 300 yards (270m) away – and Steps of Lindos, which is about three quarters of a mile (1km) away. The hotel's popular 'Akrogiali' taverna/restaurant is open all day and offers a range of snacks and meals. Breakfast is served either in the taverna or out on the patio. Grade B.

Lindos Bay Hotel (tel: 42211/2). This large hotel is set on its own fine shingle beach, and offers a saltwater swimming-pool with sun terrace, shops, restaurant and snack bar, tennis courts and table tennis facilities, and fortnightly Greek evenings in the high season. Cots and high chairs are available on request, but on a negative note the three-sided lifts carry no warning notices of possible danger. The management operates a mini-bus service to and from Líndhos several times a day. Grade A.

Lindos Sun Hotel (tel: 31453). Situated five minutes' walk from a stretch of dark, coarse sand, this is a small, friendly hotel offering lovely sea and mountain views. However, the walk to Líndhos is up a steep road, making this an unsuitable choice for those with walking difficulties. Facilities include a large, freshwater swimming-pool with poolside bar. Grade B.

Hotel Steps of Lindos (tel: 42262). Located about ten minutes' walk down a fairly steep hill to a sand-and-shingle stretch of beach, the many traditionally-styled three-storey accommodation blocks of the hotel are set into a hillside, affording magnificent views across Vliha Bay. Facilities include stylishly furnished and comfortable public rooms, a lounge/reception area, main lounge bar opening on to a terrace, outdoor swimming-pool set in sun terraces, separate children's pool, a poolside bar/restaurant, and shops selling newspapers, souvenirs and jewellery. For children the amenities range from a paddling pool and playground, to high chairs, free cots, and babysitting on request. For those who enjoy sport there is a tennis court, table tennis, and various watersports near by, including waterskiing, windsurfing and pedaloes. The hotel has a quiet, relaxing atmosphere, making it suitable for families and older couples. Guests here also need to be fit, since there are numerous steps to negotiate – and no lifts. Grade A.

Restaurants and Entertainment

Líndhos offers a large selection of tavernas, restaurants and lively bars to suit all tastes. The **Taverna Mihalis**, located near the ancient theatre, specialises in grilled meat and chicken, and has a pleasant rooftop terrace, while the **Lindian Apollo** cafeteria/pub, which also has an attractive roof garden, offers a variety of cocktails

LÍNDHOS

Eye-catching local pottery

including some with startling names – 'Slow Screw' and 'Screaming Orgasm'. The **Antika** cocktail bar is spacious and stylishly furnished. There are also a couple of discos, situated on the outskirts of the village.

Shopping

Líndhos is famous for its pottery, especially plates, which make excellent wall decorations and good souvenirs. Lindhian pottery was first made in the 16th century AD. It is said that the Knights of St John captured a ship carrying Persian craftsmen and held them on Rhodes, where they taught the art of pottery. The best plates were made in the 16th and 17th centuries, as is shown from the large number of examples on display in the Benaki Museum, Athens.

Other Facilities

Bank: the National Bank is close to the main square, off Odhos Acropolis. (Open: Mondays to Thursdays 09.00–14.00hrs; Friday 09.00–13.30hrs; Saturday, 09.00–13.30hrs.)

Buses: the main square serves as the bus terminal.

Clinic: to the left of Odhos Acropolis, opposite the donkey park (tel: 31224).

Ferry-boats: a scheduled excursion boat departs from Grand Harbour Bay daily at 14.30hrs for Rhodes City.

Police: at the further end of Odhos Acropolis.

Post Office: close to the donkey marshalling yard on Odhos Acropolis, near the main square.

Toilets: a public lavatory is located by the main square.

Tourist Office: in Platia Eleftherios, the main square. (Open: daily 09.00–13.00hrs and 17.00–20.00hrs.)

OTHER RESORTS AND SITES

◆◆
AFÁNDOU
east coast

Afándou means 'hidden place' or 'invisible' and it is indeed set back some way from the coast. It is a pleasant resort, much quieter and more select than Falirakion or Ixós. However, buses run from the village along the coast road and there are taxis. Afándou retains a traditional village atmosphere, and you will see locals sipping ouzo and playing backgammon outside the tavernas there. The beach is a fairly peaceful stretch of coarse sand and shingle, with secluded rocky inlets. Beach umbrellas and sunbeds are readily available. A handful of tavernas and bars can be found along the main road. Afándou is particularly popular with golfers, since it has an excellent 18-hole golf course.

Accommodation
Hotel Golden Days (tel: 516519). This simple, unsophisticated family-run hotel, built in 1986, stands just outside the village and enjoys lovely countryside and sea views. Amenities include a small reception area combined with a lounge/bar and a breakfast room.

Xenia Golf (tel: 51121). An attractive, 52-bed hotel in the golf course grounds and bordering the beach. It offers no fewer than three swimming-pools. Grade B.

There is a reasonable selection of tavernas as well as several coffee shops and a bakery around the village square.

◆◆◆
ARKHÁNGELOS (Archangelos)
east coast, 20 miles (33km) from Rhodes Town

This is the largest village on the island and, although not overly attractive, is pleasantly situated within the principal citrus-growing region on the island. It is worth visiting if only for the potteries here which specialise in hand-thrown ceramics, especially plates, and for the hand-made leather boots. The village, on the coast road, lies in the shadow of a ruined 15th-century fortress commissioned by Grand Knight Master Orsini. There are three churches and the village contains an interesting and atmospheric old quarter in which you can still find cobblers producing the leather boots originally worn as protection against snakes. Women's boots appear to be made in two pieces – the top half overlaps the instep and ankle giving the impression that there is a separate boot or shoe beneath. In fact the boots are all one piece, the true length coming to well above the knee, with the surplus pulled down in a fold over the ankle as far as the base of the heel. They are made of tough, hard-working hide or very soft goatskin. Surrounding Arkhángelos are numerous orange groves, while lemons and limes, mandarins and grapes also flourish.

Accommodation
Accommodation includes the modern, Grade-B **Hotel Fivros**, set in large, peaceful gardens on the edge of the village; and the Grade-E **Hotel Arkhangelos**.

RHODES (RÓDHOS)

RESORTS

♦♦♦
EPTA PIYES (Seven Springs)
*about 18 miles (30km) from
Rhodes Town*

Just off the main east coast road
leading to Líndhos, Epta Piyes is
one of the island's premier
beauty spots – a pleasant place
with an Italian-made lake fed by
seven streams, and a waterfall.

Peace and quiet at Epta Piyes

Not surprisingly, it is a popular
destination with excursion
groups. To reach the lake you
can take either a woodland trail
or walk through a long, narrow,
stream-running tunnel – an odd
and unusual experience, and
not one to be recommended to
those suffering from
claustrophobia; the tunnel is
pitch-black, and the traffic
two-way and chaotic. It is safe to
swim in the lake, but
inadvisable to get too close to
the wall of the dam.

Restaurant
There is a restaurant,
specialising in charcoal grills,
some of whose tables are
supported on flat-topped rocks
in and alongside the water, all
set in prolifically wooded
countryside.

♦♦♦
FALIRAKION
*northeastern coast, about 9 miles
(15km) from Rhodes Town*

A long sweep of coarse, grey
sand sloping gently to the sea is
undoubtedly what has turned
Falirakion into one of Rhodes'
liveliest and most popular
summer resorts – a far cry from
the small fishing village it once
was. Falirakion offers plenty to
keep visitors occupied both on
and off the beach. Sunbathing is
good, swimming is safe, and the
wide selection of watersports
available include windsurfing,
parascending, waterskiing,
jet-skiing and pedaloes. The
resort also offers a mini-golf
course and a go-kart track. The
beach can – and, indeed usually
does – get crowded in high
season near the village, but a
short walk further along will
bring you to a quieter spot. As
well as innumerable large
hotels (with more being built),
Falirakion has plenty of seaside
amenities such as restaurants
with rooms to let, changing
cabins, showers, deck-chairs
and parasols.

Accommodation
Falirakion contains a number of
huge hotel complexes, such as
the **Esperides Beach**, **Blue Sea**
and **Rodos Beach**, which border
the beach. At the far end of the
bay are several smaller, more
Greek-style establishments,
together with a number of
self-catering villas which, it
should be noted, are located on
the wrong side of the very busy
main road.
Hotel Apollo Beach (tel: 85251,
85513). Standing in its own fresh,

Stretching out – Falirakion beach

green gardens right beside Falirakion's gently shelving sandy beach, and next door to the Faliraki Beach Hotel, this somewhat impersonal, 293-room establishment is close to the resort's tavernas and discos. It offers comfortable accommodation and good food, even if overall standards have declined slightly in recent years. Amenities include an outdoor freshwater pool, sun terraces, lounge, television and card rooms, bar, restaurant serving table d'hôte and à la carte dishes, taverna, hairdressing and beauty salons, and a gift shop. There are tennis courts with equipment for hire, a sauna, table tennis and billiards. For children there is a swimming-pool, playground, high chair and cots, and baby-sitting on request. Grade A.
Hotel Blue Sea (tel: 85512). This 302-room hotel stands about a mile (1.6km) from the village. It has comfortable rooms, a good reputation for food and service, and gardens which border a lovely wide stretch of sand and pebble beach. A regular bus service to Rhodes Town stops outside the hotel. Amenities include outdoor and indoor swimming-pools, jacuzzi, three lounges, bar, two tennis courts, squash court, pool table, live music three nights a week and a regular Greek night, shops, and a hairdresser. There is also a children's pool and small playground. Grade A.
Hotel Calypso (tel: 85623). Step through the gardens of the stylish Calypso and you are right on Falirakion's beach. The attractive terraces are equally inviting to sunbathers, and there

is a good sized children's pool and play area. Other features include a saltwater swimming-pool with poolside snackbar; tennis court and crazy-golf course; games room with billiards table; weekly discothèque and fortnightly Greek evenings; shops; beauty salon; sauna and gymnasium. The hotel's disadvantage is that it is in a somewhat isolated position, about 25 minutes' walk from the centre of the resort, but to compensate it is very smartly furnished and decorated and well recommended. Grade A. **Hotel Colossos Beach** (tel: 85502). This hotel is a good choice for families, offering a

wealth of facilities including its own stretch of private sand-and-shingle beach. Situated just over two miles (3km) from the centre of Falirakion, the hotel features a lounge, three bars, television room with satellite programmes, shops, a hairdressing salon, beauty salon, a main swimming-pool and a children's pool, surrounded by terraces, extensive gardens, a poolside bar, and a beach bar. There are two restaurants offering a choice of menus, a cafeteria, à la carte taverna, and self-service poolside restaurant. There is dancing most nights in the 'Ace' discothèque, with regular live-music sessions, and frequent Greek evenings are held in the taverna. There is also a programme of games and

Parasols at Falirakion: splashes of colour before a splash in the sea

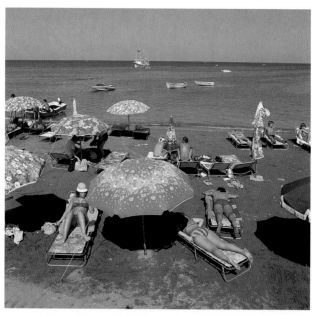

competitions. Visitors with children should note that the lifts here are of the potentially dangerous, three-sided variety. Grade A.

Esperides Beach (tel: 85503). Dominating popular Falirakion bay and surrounded by a huge garden, this is a large, modern, highly recommended complex that includes three swimming-pools, restaurant, cocktail bar, lounge, bridge room, television room, taverna, snack bar and discothèque. There is also a mini-market, hairdressing salon, car/bicycle rental office, and an excellent children's playground – one of the best on the island. The hotel is situated about 30 minutes' walk from the centre of Falirakion, but compensates for its somewhat isolated position with a very lively entertainment programme that includes party nights and Greek evenings. Its excellent facilities are marred slightly by the use of three-sided lifts. Grade A.

Esperos Palace Hotel (tel: 85742). Situated right on the beach, the stylish and elegant Esperos Palace has earned a reputation as one of the best hotels in Rhodes since its opening in 1985. Set in extensive gardens, it is linked by a bridge in the grounds to its sister hotel, Esperides Beach, whose facilities are shared. The hotel's 397 rooms are in two blocks connected by an art gallery corridor, and all are air-conditioned and have balconies with sea or garden views, larger-than-average bathrooms, self-dialling telephones, and mini-fridges. Facilities include two swimming-pools with sun terraces, gardens, a piano bar, lounge bar, snack bar, boutique, mini-market and à la carte restaurant. There are also two tennis courts, squash courts, mini-golf course, and facilities for billiards. Grade A.

Faliraki Beach Hotel (tel: 85301). Recently renovated, this impressive and attractive hotel stands in a good position right in front of Faliraki's wide beach, reached through attractive gardens. Bars, tavernas and restaurants are all around, and shops, buses and taxis less than a minute's walk away. The resort centre is five minutes' walk away. Hotel facilities include a large outdoor swimming-pool, sun terraces with chairs and umbrellas, poolside bar, lounge, bar, card room, restaurant, à la carte taverna and hairdressing salon. Occasional Greek evenings are held by the pool side or in the bar, and for sports enthusiasts the hotel has two tennis courts, with equipment for hire, table tennis and putting, and there is golf available at Afándou, about four miles (6.5km) away. Children have their own pool and small playground, and high chairs, cots and early meals are available. Grade A.

Faliro Hotel (tel: 26511). For those on a budget, this small hotel is extremely popular, mainly thanks to the hospitality shown by Yiannis, his wife and their three children who make guests feel part of the family. There are tavernas and shops practically on the doorstep, the beach is about five minutes' walk away, and there is a bus stop close by for trips into Rhodes Town. Breakfast is served on the outside terraced area of the bar. Grade D.

Pension Nefeli (tel: 85658). Another popular choice with those on a tight budget, the Nefeli is a small but pleasant property situated in a central position close to local shops, bars and tavernas and only ten minutes' stroll from a good stretch of beach. Facilities include a bar, lounge, and breakfast room. Grade C.

Hotel Rodos Beach (tel: 85471). This attractive and well-maintained hotel has a reputation for friendly service. Situated by the beach, where waterskiing and windsurfing are available in high season, it is just over a mile (1.6km) from Falirakion village. The comfortable, well-furnished bedrooms are in either the main building or bungalows in the hotel's large and pleasant gardens which border the beach. There is a saltwater swimming-pool with sun terrace, poolside taverna with à la carte menu, beach bar, free tennis and table tennis, nightly discothèque, shops and hairdressing salon and a children's pool and playground. Three-sided lifts are used here, carrying warnings that children must be accompanied by an adult. Grade A.

Hotel Sun Palace (tel: 85650). This is a good quality hotel enjoying a relatively quiet location along a flat road about 20 minutes' walk from the resort centre and about 10 minutes' walk from the beach across a busy road. Facilities include a large, Olympic-sized freshwater swimming-pool set in sun terraces, a poolside bar, principal bar, modern lounge areas and a card room. The hotel offers two restaurants featuring a weekly à la carte lunchtime poolside buffet and weekly buffet-style dinners, and regular entertainment ranges from Greek nights to discos. Other facilities include tennis courts, mini-golf and table tennis. Three-sided lifts here carry no warnings, and there are no depth markings in the swimming-pool. Grade A.

Restaurants and Entertainment

As in most seaside resorts, the road that leads down to the beach is where you will find the majority of the bars, tavernas, snack bars and shops. Although menus tend to cater more for international tastes, traditional cuisine can still be enjoyed at a few places. The **Acrogiali** Greek taverna bordering the beach has a good selection of Greek speciality dishes, including moussaka and squid. **Chaplin's Bar**, near by, is very lively in the evenings, and the popular cocktail bars include **Falirala** and **Blue Waves**, both near the beach, and the **Bianco Bar**, on the approach road.

Nightlife in Falirakion is very lively. From sunset the bars in the main street are packed with people – usually youngsters – enjoying themselves drinking and listening to the latest sounds. The most popular discothèques are **Buskers**, which has a weekly toga party, and **The Set**, just as lively but with a slightly more sophisticated atmosphere.

♦♦♦
IALYSSOS
about 6 miles (10km) southwest of Rhodes Town

The ancient city of Ialyssos occupies a plateau at the top of the 876-foot (267m) high Mount Filerimos, near the small but fast-developing west coast resort of Triánda. According to myth, the city was founded by Ialyssos, the third of the three grandsons of the sun god Helios. The earliest settlers here were the Phoenicians followed by the Mycenaean Achaeans, who arrived from the Greek mainland about 1450BC and named the place Achaea. The Dorians, under whom it grew to a city-state equalling Líndhos and Kamiros in importance, named it after its mythical founder.

With a commanding view of the island and the coast, the site has an obvious strategic value. Some time during the Dorian period the city began to edge down the western slopes of the

Fresco, Ayios Georgios, Ialyssos

RESORTS

Church of Our Lady of Filerimos

hill towards Kremastí and Triánda. In this area an enormous necropolis containing numerous tombs was excavated by the French archaeologist Salzmann and British consul Biliotti between 1859 and 1871. They unearthed many finds now on display in museums throughout the world. In 1914 and again between 1929 and 1932 the Italians Majuri and Jacopi, in the course of fresh excavations, unearthed more new graves with rich finds from the Archaic, Classical and Hellenistic periods.

The Knights of St John built a monastery and a church at Ialyssos. The monastery one sees today – with a courtyard surrounded by cells – was rebuilt by the Italians.

What to See

Chapel of Ayios Georgios

Almost every inch of wall space in this small, subterranean Byzantine church is covered with frescos of the 14th and 15th centuries. Some have been removed to reveal part of a Christian cross carved in stone beneath the plaster. Among the most interesting of the frescos are a sequence of Grand Masters Kneeling Before Christ, a St George, and also a well preserved series of incidents in the life of Christ which compose the decoration of the barrel vault.

Church of Our Lady of Filerimos

This is the first building most visitors to Ialyssos encounter after leaving the car park. Heavily restored after World War II, it was built on a site occupied, successively, by a Phoenician temple, a 3rd-century BC Doric temple to Athena Polias, an Early Christian basilica, a Catholic church converted from an Orthodox original, a restored 20th-century version of the church, and finally the present-day restoration. The chapel, built by d'Aubusson when he was the Knights' Grand Master, leads to two smaller chapels. On the floor of the rear of the church is a little red mosaic fish, part of the floor of the original, Early Christian building. There are two altars in the adjacent chapels, one for Catholic, the other for Orthodox worship, but only the latter is used today.

Cloisters
Beyond the church are the courtyards, galleries and cloisters of the monastery, somewhat heavily restored during the Italian occupation of Rhodes this century. The monks' cells are distinguished from one another by tiled plaques, each depicting a different flower.

Doric Fountain
Over the crest of the hill to the right of the monastery entrance, a flight of steps leads down to a 4th-century Classical fountain screened by a row of Doric columns, and discovered by accident in 1926. Once considered a sacred spring, it has since dried up. The Italians

Icons in Golgothas recall the Passion

restored two of the six columns which had supported the roof of the portico and which was damaged by a landslide.

Stations of the Cross
A tree-lined avenue leading from the car park, and known as Golgothas, is lined on one side with 14 copper icons representing the stations of the cross, erected during the Italian occupation. At the end of the avenue, steps lead to a circular vantage point commanding breathtaking views along the coast. A mass of flowers in summer make it a popular spot with photographers.
A souvenir and drinks kiosk on the edge of the car park sells the liqueur Sette Erbe (Seven Herbs), which is made by monks.

Temple of Athena and Zeus Polias
Dating from the 3rd century BC, this Doric temple runs north and south in front of the Church of Our Lady of Filerimos. Foundations, bases, stumps of fluted pillars are all there, but little else. The temple was similar in style to the temple of Athena at Líndhos, but much larger.
Open: daily 08.30–17.00hrs. Closed Mondays.

Accommodation
Hotel Blue Horizon (tel: 93484). Commanding magnificent sea views, with the Turkish coast on the horizon, the hotel is well located on a stretch of sand and shingle beach, reached through well tended lawns and gardens. The large gardens contain a swimming-pool and sun terraces, while other hotel facilities include a restaurant,

RESORTS

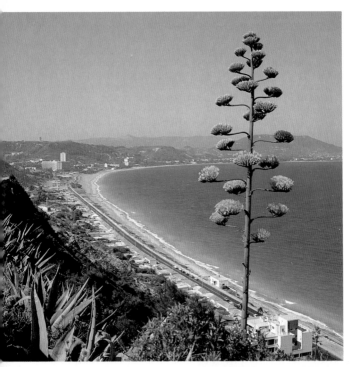

Ixós – miles of sand, sea and surf

lounge, bar, snack bar, television and card room, shop, and hairdressing salon. Regular Greek folklore evenings are staged, while for children there is a separate pool and a playground. High chairs are available, as are early meals if a sufficient number of children are staying. Grade A.

Other hotel accommodation can be found in nearby **Triánda** (see separate entry).

Restaurant
The **Sandy Beach** taverna/coffee bar serves Greek dishes, with barbecued meat and fish as particular specialities.

IXÓS (Ixia)
northwest coast
The lively, highly developed resort of Ixós is less than three miles (5km) along the main road from Rhodes Town, and separated from it only by the headland known as Monte Smith. It is tailor-made for the young, with countless bars, tavernas, cafeterias, discos and nightclubs packing this stretch of coastline and offering almost non-stop entertainment. Ixós enjoys a near constant breeze, making even the hottest days

feel comfortable. At times the wind can become very fresh, though umbrellas to act as wind-breaks are available for hire. Being only three miles (5km) from the island's airport, the resort does suffer from some aircraft noise, but this generally is not sufficiently annoying to detract from the enjoyment of a holiday here.

There are excellent facilities on the long, narrow beach of dark sand, shingle and pebble, with windsurfing particularly to be recommended from all the watersports on offer. Pedaloes are also available for hire, as are jet-skis, yachts and motor boats. The road along this stretch of the coast is busy most of the day, making it important to watch for children's safety, and the sea itself is not as calm as on the east coast.

Snacks, freshwater showers and sunbeds are all available on the beach, which is especially popular with early morning joggers. The resort also offers a children's playground, while several hotels have good sports facilities, including tennis courts, mini-golf courses and table tennis.

Accommodation

Avra Beach Hotel (tel: 25284/25308). Surrounded by a large garden, the hotel offers a wealth of amenities that range from a small shopping centre to children's swimming-pool, kindergarten, hairdresser, car rental office, restaurant, open bar, and discothèque. Grade A.

Bel Air Hotel (tel: 23731). Situated at the foot of a wooded slope just back from the main road leading into the resort, with a stretch of beach opposite. The somewhat shabby hotel (despite its grading) has a swimming-pool, dining room, lounge, bars, games for children, a tennis court, and a shop. Potentially dangerous three-sided lifts are used here. Grade A.

Cosmopolitan Hotel (tel: 35373). This new hotel is positioned across the road from the seafront and only a short walk from the resort's beach. The centre of Ixós is a ten-minute walk away. A feature of the hotel is a huge, freshwater swimming-pool flanked by spacious sun terraces, and there is also a separate pool for children. The attractive public areas include an excellent lounge and bar. Early suppers and children's menus are available. Grade A.

Hotel Dionysos (tel: 23021/5). A sprawling complex of three buildings, the Dionysos is situated three minutes from the beach, well back from the busy coast road, and offers spacious grounds together with two large pools – one with a children's section – poolside bar and gardens, and a children's playground. Other facilities include a 300-seat cinema and two bars. Notices warn of the possible danger posed by the hotel's three-sided lifts. Grade A.

Hotel Elina (tel: 92466). The Elina is particularly popular with Dutch and German visitors to the island. Standing in extensive grounds which border the sand-and-pebble beach, about 25 minutes' walk from the resort

RESORTS

centre and about three miles (5km) along the coast from Rhodes Town, it has a spacious reception lobby with comfortable lounge area; bar; card tables; shops; a hairdressing salon; a large swimming-pool set in extensive sun terraces and lawns; and a poolside bar with self-service snacks available at lunchtimes. Most bedrooms have pleasant sea views. For toddlers, cots are available as are high chairs and children's menus. Grade A.

Hotel Lito (tel: 23511/23512). This modern, 97-room hotel, located in the centre of Ixós opposite a stretch of shingle beach, is a particular favourite with British visitors. Facilities include a freshwater swimming-pool surrounded by extensive sun-bathing terraces, an attractive restaurant, and a lively bar. Disadvantages include the fact that some rooms are subject to noise from an adjacent taverna, and some of the sea-view bedrooms suffer from traffic noise. The three-sided lifts used here have warning signs and emergency buttons. Grade B.

Hotel Metropolitan Capsis (tel: 25015). An impressive, well-designed hotel surrounded by spacious gardens and sunny terraces, the 693-room Metropolitan Capsis offers a choice of lounges, bars, a card room, hairdresser's, shops, two swimming-pools, a terrace snack bar and a taverna. There is also a children's playground and a well-equipped nursery for toddlers under the age of six. Dancing is a regular feature in the hotel's 'Roof Garden'

discothèque, and an extensive entertainments programme includes fashion shows, games, Greek evenings and video shows. For the active there are two tennis courts, a games room with table tennis and billiards, aerobics, and basketball and volleyball courts. Grade A.

Miramare Beach (tel: 24251). This is a complex of luxury bungalows, all with sea views, set amid well tended gardens packed with trees, and situated close to a 1,000-metre/yard long stretch of beach. The hotel's restaurant is noted for its cuisine, and there is a pleasant piano bar situated next to the swimming-pool. Deluxe grade.

Oceanis Hotel (tel: 24881). This well located hotel enjoys an excellent reputation for its cuisine, both international and Greek. Situated across the busy coast road from a stretch of shingle beach, it is within ten minutes' walk of the centre of Ixós, and three miles (5km) from Rhodes Town. Recently refurbished, it offers a medium-sized seawater swimming-pool, spacious public areas and, for children, high chairs, early meals and children's menus. Guests with youngsters should note that the swimming-pool carries no depth markings. Grade A.

Hotel Olympic Palace (tel: 28755). The hotel offers an impressive range of amenities and facilities for visitors of all ages. Situated opposite its own private, gently sloping sand-and-pebble beach – reached across the busy main road – it has an outdoor swimming-pool set in well equipped sun terraces and pretty gardens; an indoor swimming-pool; poolside snack bar; spacious lounges; card and television rooms; a women's hairdressing salon; and various shops. For children there is a paddling pool, playground, cots, high chairs, babysitting, and early dinners on request. Meals in the hotel's main restaurant offer a choice of international dishes, with waiter service for both lunch and dinner. The 'Aegean' nightclub features a disco most evenings as well as regular Greek evenings. Live entertainment is provided regularly in the main bar. Sports facilities include a tennis court, mini-golf, games room with table tennis and video games, a gymnasium, and bicycle rental. Although it is officially classified as deluxe, standards have tended to decline slightly in recent years.

Relaxing by the Rodos Palace pool

Rodos Bay Hotel (tel: 23661). Beautifully tucked into the side of pine-covered hills, the Rodos Bay offers stunning views from its top floor/terraces. Ixós beach is reached via a tunnel under the main road, and the centre of the resort is a 20-minute walk away. The hotel's rooftop outdoor swimming-pool has a poolside bar for drinks and snacks. Other amenities include gardens, shops, a hairdressing salon, television/video room, lounges, restaurant, two bars and a sauna. Barbecues featuring Greek dancing are held regularly, as are live music sessions in the taverna. There is also a nightclub, tennis court and table tennis facilities. Children have their own separate freshwater pool. Grade A.

Rodos Palace Hotel and Apartments (tel: 25222). The Rodos Palace is a tall building facing out over the beach and sea. The complex consists of a large, modern luxury hotel and blocks of apartments, studios and bungalows dotted among the gardens. During the day, as an alternative to the beach, guests can relax around the spacious indoor and outdoor swimming-pools. The hotel offers a selection of restaurants, bars, lounges and shops, a sauna, hairdressing salon and, for sports enthusiasts, table tennis, mini-golf, three tennis courts, crazy-golf, volleyball, waterpolo and a games room with electronic games. Entrance to the hotel's 'Club Tropicana' discothèque is free. Children's needs are well catered for, with a pool of their own and a playground. Early suppers can be served in bedrooms, and cots and high chairs are available. Deluxe grade.

Restaurants and Entertainment
There are few restaurants in Ixós offering genuine Greek food, most specialising in foreign dishes such as smorgasbord, burgers, pizzas and spaghetti. A varied selection of international and Greek dishes, however, is offered at the **Sea House** pub/restaurant, right on the beach. Nightlife in Ixós is plentiful. Restaurants and tavernas that line the main coastal road bustle with activity, and many – such as the **Delfinia** – even have live music. Ixós is also the site of one of Rhodes' most popular disco-thèques, **Hi-Way**. Though pricey, the light show is sophisticated and the music up-to-the-minute. At the **PlayBoy** disco, you will find one of the most talented disc jockeys on the island.

Shopping
For shopping, Ixós has a reasonable selection of establishments – sufficient to satisfy most holidaymakers' needs – but Rhodes town itself is a better bet, and easily and inexpensively reached by bus or taxi.

◆◆◆
KAMIROS

northwest coast, about 21 miles (34km) from Rhodes Town

Kamiros (sometimes spelled Kameiros) is the one of the three ancient cities of Rhodes, and well worth visiting, not least for its delightful position on a gentle slope looking down to the sea. Abandoned at about the time of Christ, it is one of the best preserved of Classical Greek towns, with houses rising each side of a central street leading upwards from a newly excavated area, mainly of 3rd-century BC buildings.

Built on successively ascending terraces on a fertile hill, it is believed that the site was inhabited from the prehistoric period. Evidence indicates it flourished before the island's colonisation by the Dorians although, because of its unprotected situation by the sea, it did not attain the prominence of its sister towns of Líndhos and Ialyssos. However, it continued to be inhabited until the 4th century AD, when it appears to have been mysteriously abandoned. It was rediscovered in 1859 by Salzmann and Biliotti who carried out extensive excavations, uncovering a cemetery which yielded numerous finds now on display in the British Museum in London. These include a small terracotta basket of fruit, a metal cup containing hen's eggs, and a terracotta figure of a woman kneading dough. Much more major excavation work was carried out after 1929 by Italian architects, whose work was interrupted by the war. Thankfully, work has restarted.

The ancient city of Kamiros

RESORTS

What to See

In its heyday the city spread out over a valley, with the unfortified acropolis on the highest point to the south. On the acropolis, which is approximately 400 feet (120m) above sea-level, were found archaic statues now on display in the Museum of Rhodes (Arkheologikó Mousío) in Rhodes Town. Here, too, stood a Temple of Athena Polias, of which only the foundations remain. The temple was built in the 6th or 5th century BC, then restored and added to later on during the Hellenistic period (3rd–2nd centuries BC).

In front was a 650-foot (200m) long, Doric stoa, or walkway, six columns of which were restored by the Italians but have since toppled over. An enormous cistern (6th-century BC) can be seen outside the stoa. A narrow path ran along most of the length of this, and beyond here was the public area of the market square.

The area of the city occupied by private houses, which has already been excavated, spreads out to the north of the acropolis, although it represents only part of the total area. Some of the houses are reasonably well preserved, and feature interior courtyards surrounded by a colonnade. Most private houses are from the Hellenistic period.

Several travel agents organise excursions to Kamiros, which can also be reached by bus from Mandraki Harbour, Rhodes Town.
Open: daily 08.30–17.00hrs. Closed Mondays.

◆◆◆
KAMIROS SKALA

About 10 miles (16km) to the south of the ancient city is Kamiros Skala, once the busy harbour for the inland town of Kritinía, originally a Cretan settlement. Today it is a delightful, sleepy little harbour complete with colourful fishing boats and a couple of bar-restaurants specialising, not surprisingly, in fish. The best is probably **Althemenis**, which has a delightful terrace bordering the sea.

In the high season summer months a boat takes passengers through a group of offshore islands to **Khálki** (see page opposite), whose harbour and pleasant seaside capital are understandably beginning to attract visitors from Rhodes.

Close to Kamiros Skala is **Kastellos**, an impressive ruined fortress, built by the Knights of St John, and reached by a loop off the main road. The Knights were attracted by the site's strategic position commanding nearly 50 miles (80km) of the western coastline, and they built the castle on a grand scale. The fortress is worth visiting for the views alone – not only of the coastline and sea, but even landward, where Mount Atáviros dominates.

◆◆
KATTAVÍA

about 60 miles (96km) south of Rhodes Town

This small village, almost at the southern tip of Rhodes, consists of a couple of shops and a few tavernas with a pleasant local atmosphere, especially in the

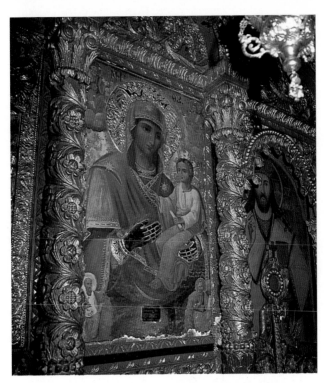

evenings. The village church is noted for its frescos. The magnificent beach at nearby **Prasonísi** is reached by a five-mile (8km) track, creating an isthmus connecting the mainland with the 'island' of Prasonísi, or Leak Island. This beach is excellent for windsurfing, but there are no organised facilities apart from a small but usually lively taverna. The nearby beaches at **Apolakkiá** and **Monólithos** provide good seclusion at any time of the year, and the surrounding countryside offers plenty of interest for walkers.

Painted icon, Kattavía church

◆◆◆
KHÁLKI

off the northwest coast of Rhodes

Khálki is a mountainous little island, the sort of place you could either love or hate. It offers a quiet, relaxing style of life with absolutely nothing to do except stroll across a rather barren landscape to a good sandy beach or a number of sandy coves; explore a ruined village, from where there are good views of Rhodes and other nearby islands; or eat at one of

RESORTS

the small selection of tavernas along the attractive harbourside. Here you can get to know some of the locals who, through years of emigration, now have strong family ties in many parts of the world, especially America and Australia.

Niborio, the chief village, is sited round the harbour. Although there are no hotels, accommodation is available in private houses and there are bungalows by the sea. The nearest beach is Pandemos Beach, a ten-minute walk on the other side of the hill behind the town.

Chora, 2½ miles (4km) from Niborio, was a flourishing centre in the 18th and 19th centuries but the hilltop town is now practically deserted. The medieval castle with the ruins of a church behind it offers a magnificent view from its location above the village.

If you decide to stay on the island you should be prepared to put up with the very real probability of interruptions to the local fresh water supplies, as Khálki relies almost totally on water being delivered by boat from the mainland. But if you can cope with this, you should find the island ideal for a week or a few days' relaxation away from it all.

The boat trip to Khálki from Kamiros Skala on the west coast of Rhodes takes one and a half hours, with daily sailings scheduled at 15.00hrs. However, times vary at the discretion of the boat owners, so it is wise to check in advance. Cost of the journey is negotiable with the boat owners.

◆◆
KHARÁKION
east coast

The fishing village and resort of Kharákion is built round an attractive crescent-shaped bay, with a fine shingle and sand beach offering crystal-clear swimming and excellent snorkelling. It has been a popular lunchtime, weekend and holiday spot with Greeks for some time, so tavernas in the bay offer excellent fish. **Argo's** is probably the best, though it is not cheap. Visitors can enjoy watching the fish being unloaded from the colourful caïques as they return from night fishing trips in the early mornings.

The village is overlooked by ruined **Feraklos Castle**, occupying an extensive flat area on a hilltop. The castle was built by the Knights of St John and was one of their most powerful fortresses. It was used as a jailhouse for both war and civil prisoners, and was one of the last castles on the island to fall to the invading Turks in the 16th century. To the north are the remains of ancient tombs and a church which is decorated with frescos of the 15th and 17th centuries. A road runs through orange and lemon groves to the village of **Másari**, about one and a half miles (2.5km) away, while the superb sandy bay of **Agathi**, one of the island's best, is a 25-minute walk to the north.

Accommodation
Accommodation in Khárakion is in self-catering rooms and apartments.

Fishing boat moored in Kolimbia cove

◆◆
KOLIMBIA
east coast

A long shady avenue of eucalyptus trees, lined by a handful of pensions and tavernas, leads down from the busy main Rhodes Town–Líndhos road to Kolimbia's sand and shingle beach. Here you will find several tavernas and bars, watersports, sunbeds and umbrellas. Near by is a smaller cove with fishing boats and a taverna as well as a tiny fishing harbour. At present Kolimbia is a relatively unspoiled and charming spot – even if the beach itself is somewhat ordinary – but a considerable amount of building work is taking place designed to transform it into one of the island's major resorts.

At the heart of the village is a large square containing homes for the aged. To the left a road runs about two miles (3km) through the avenue of eucalyptus trees down to the sea. Along this road, in a peach grove, lie the remains of a 6th-century AD basilica and some mosaic flooring, hidden among grasses and with walls no more than three feet (1m) high. Continuing along the road, you reach a fork. The path to the right takes you to a fine sandy beach below a rise; the left fork leads to a small cove with a jetty, a restaurant, and a long sand-and-shingle beach particularly suitable for children because of the shallowness of the water near the shore. Waterskis, windsurfers and pedaloes can all be rented and are generally in good condition. Kolimbia enjoys easy access to Falirakion, Rhodes Town and Líndhos, while the airport is about 25 miles (40km) away.

Accommodation
Irene Palace (tel: 56224). Situated in a quiet area close to Kolimbia, this is a well maintained, family-run hotel

RESORTS

offering 188 rooms, most with a terrace and all with private facilities. Cots and baby-sitting are available on request. There is a large freshwater swimming-pool surrounded by gardens and lawns and a separate children's pool as well as a children's playground on a grassy surface. Exterior public areas are spacious and relaxing, and the hotel staff friendly and helpful. Buffet breakfasts and lunches are served in the snack bar, and dinner is also a buffet, with four courses. Early meals and children's menus are available on request. Entertainment consists of organised games, a Happy Hour, bingo, and party evenings. Grade A.

Apart from this hotel, other holiday accommodation is available in small, unpretentious hotels or numerous studios and apartments.

Restaurants
The choice of restaurants and bars in Kolimbia is limited. The best of those that do exist is probably the beachside **Nissaki**, which has a shady, vine-covered terrace and another terrace bordering the sea.

◆◆
KREMASTÍ
west coast, about 8 miles (13km) from Rhodes Town
The blossoming resort of Kremastí may not be the ideal choice for those in search of trendy night spots. Nevertheless, in the evenings the resort livens up, with the accent on traditional Greek entertainment in the numerous bars and tavernas. Life centres round the main street, lined by tavernas, small shops and cafés – the kind of place where you

The church of Our Lady of Kremastí

can still get a real village *souvláki* (kebab). The wide pebbly beach is about 10 minutes' walk from the centre of the resort, and there is a bus service to Rhodes Town and to the lively resort of Ixós, only four miles (6.5km) away.

What to See

The unusual modern church of Our Lady of Kremastí was built not *on* the site of a former church but, strangely, *around* it. The interior is worth inspecting for the pretty side chapel. Also in the village is a large modern church decorated in the Byzantine style which was paid for by villagers who had emigrated to the US. The interior is very richly decorated. The village celebrates in ancient style the festival of the **Assumption of the Virgin**, one of the most important festivals of the Dodecanese. The actual date is 15 August, but the celebrations last from 14 to 23 August, including a large-scale flea-market, fiesta and funfare. In the necropolis around Kremastí were found several examples of Geometric and Archaic vases which are now on display in the Archaeological Museum in Rhodes Town.

Accommodation

Places to stay are simple and unsophisticated, mostly village rooms and studios.

Restaurants

The **International** bar/restaurant is popular with late-night revellers, while nearby **Mike's** snack bar/cafeteria offers a good selection of dishes – though the music tends to be on the loud side!

◆◆◆
LÁRDHOS
southeast coast
Lárdhos is an attractive, small but developing village popular with those looking for a chance to unwind and sample Greek life. In the colourful village square there is a fountain of spa water, a reasonable choice of shops for those catering for themselves, and a variety of reasonably priced tavernas. The imposing Italian architecture here is a legacy of Mussolini's day. From the village you can embark on one of a series of lovely walks through olive and lemon groves to places such as **Pévka** with its attractive sand-and-shingle beach and tavernas. One of the island's two camp sites is located at Lárdhos, and the bay below has miles of shingle and sand-dunes.

Restaurants and Entertainment

You can get a plate of delicious mixed seafood at **Maria's Restaurant**, in the main square, while nearby **Niko's Taverna** specialises in grilled dishes of pork, lamb and chicken as well as hamburgers. **Memories** cocktail bar has a good selection of drinks, a smart terrace with palm trees and plants, and a lovely roof garden.

◆◆
MONÍ THARI (Thari Monastery)
southeast Rhodes
Remotely situated 2½ miles (4km) from the village of Láerma, the monastery is, in fact, a small, domed church set in a clearing in the woods. Though it is neglected and solitary, a visit here is

recommended not least for the monastery's magnificent frescos. According to legend, Thari was founded by a Byzantine princess in thanks for the cure she obtained from the fresh woodland countryside. The north and south walls of the church contain the oldest, 12th-century, parts of the existing building, but there are some 9th-century remains in the grounds surrounding it. Of greatest interest to visitors are the fine wall paintings. Some areas of the church carry as many as four layers of paintings, and these are dated to about 1100, 1200, 1500 and 1700. Those in the apse depict the hierarchy of apostles in tones of burnt red ochre, black and cream, and there is also a group of prophets. On the right wall is a head of a horse, possibly part of a painting of St George or St Demetrius. The broad courtyard with its numerous cells is testimony to the important role the monastery once played. It can be reached by turning inland off the main road at Lárdhos (7½ miles/12km west of Líndhos) towards Láerma. From there take a turning to the left, and follow a forest road to Thari.

◆◆
MONÓLITHOS
west coast
Monólithos – the name means 'one stone' – is the site of a ruined castle dramatically perched on an isolated hill-crest and offering visitors one of the best views on the island. Not a great deal of masonry survives from the fortress built by Grand Master d'Aubusson, apart from the remains of a small chapel beside which a modern church has been built. Goat bells resound across the valleys, and the castle overlooks the round islet of Strongylo. The approach to the castle, along a stony track, is steep and hazardous, with a sheer drop down on the other side, but the resultant views are definitely worth the effort.

Monólithos castle perched on its rock

◆◆◆
PETALOUDHES (Valley of the Butterflies)
about 15 miles (25km) from Rhodes Town

A popular excursion spot, Petaloudhes (the word means 'butterflies') occupies an extensively foliaged site, steeply climbing, and complete with a pretty stream that tumbles in a series of rock pools and waterfalls. You can walk in the valley along a pathway which criss-crosses the stream and pools via rustic bridges and rock steps. Delightful though the scene is, it is not for this that hordes of tourists descend in the summer, but for the 'butterflies', which are a feature. The butterflies – which are not indigenous to the island, but native to Turkey, and are actually moths – are dark brown and cream when their wings are folded, and red, black, brown and white when in flight. They are attracted to the resin of the storax trees with which the valley abounds, and hundreds of thousands of them migrate to the valley to mate between June and the end of September each year. In recent times the numbers of butterflies have declined significantly, largely because sightseers have been frightening them into flight during the daytime (they are a nocturnal species) by clapping their hands or blowing whistles. This is now forbidden. (See also **Peace and Quiet** page 87). *Open:* daily 09.00–18.00hrs. Entrance fee. Car parking space is available.

Near Petaloudhes, and reached from the middle of the valley, where the buses stop, is the **monastery of the Virgin Mary of Kalopetra** (Moní Kalopetra). This delightful church was built in 1782 by Alexander Ypsilantis, known as the grandfather of the Greek national uprising, and a visit is well worth the upward climb.

◆◆◆
PÉVKA
east coast

If you ever wondered where families from Líndhos go for a brief escape from the invading hordes of visitors in the summer, the answer is Pévka three miles (5km) away. Once a sleepy huddle of houses amid fig orchards and vineyards, the village has grown, but is still a popular hideaway that has not yet been spoiled by over-development. The construction work now taking place, however, means that this state of affairs may not last for long, though, thankfully, the concentration is on well-designed studios and apartments that blend in well with the surroundings, rather than huge hotel complexes. What particularly attracts about Pévka is its long sandy beach sloping gently into the sea – ideal for children. Dotted with numerous small, secluded bays, there are some rocks at either end of the main beach, providing access to good snorkelling as an alternative to lazing in the sun. During the more popular months, beds, umbrellas and windsurfing boards can be hired. There are several small mini-markets in the resort where self-caterers can find most of their basic requirements, and car, moped and motorbike rentals are readily available.

Accommodation

Hotel Thalia (tel: 44508). Opened in 1989, this smart, 68-room hotel is quietly situated some ten minutes' walk from the beach. Amenities provided include a swimming-pool, small bar with large sun terrace, and breakfast room. All rooms have shower and a balcony or terrace. Grade C.

Restaurants and Entertainment

There are several good tavernas with varied menus – from fresh fish and *kalamari* to *spaghetti carbonara*. There are also half a dozen popular bars and a discothèque for revellers, sensibly soundproofed. This can be lively or quiet, depending on the season, but for swinging nightlife Líndhos is only a taxi ride or about an hour's walk away.

The **Greek House** restaurant, near the beach, specialises not surprisingly in Greek dishes including grilled and barbecued meat and fish. The **Kalari** bar has a pleasant, shady terrace, and the **Peacock** bar a roof terrace with commanding views over the bay.

◆◆◆
PROFÍTIS ILÍAS
northwest Rhodes

A winding, wooded, mountain road leads from the village of Sálakos – noted for its gardens and flowers – to the heights of Mount Profítis Ilías. Profítis Ilías is the name usually given to the highest summit on any Greek island because the prophet Elias ascended to heaven from a mountain top. On Rhodes, however, the highest summit is Atáviros, which is associated with Zeus. It is possible to drive nearly to the top of the 2,588-foot (789m) high peak of the mountain, which is heavily wooded and somewhat reminiscent of the lower Alps. Situated on the eastern and lower slopes of the mountain, the church of Ayios Nikolaos Fountoukli is worth visiting for the excellent frescos of the 14th and 15th centuries which cover the interior and which, together with the building itself, were endowed by an administrative official whose three children had died as a result of the plague. This is why the church was dedicated to St Nicholas, the protector of children. Though some of the frescos have been overpainted and touched up, they are still striking. Of particular note is one depicting St Michael bearing a huge sword, and another of a man (the donor), his wife and his three children, upholding between them the church of Christ – and the Church of St Nicholas.

Accommodation
Elafos-Elfina (tel: 22231). This chalet-style building at the

summit of the pine-clad peak would not look out of place in Switzerland. It seems to have been inspired by the surrounding forests of pungent pines. The hotel/lodge is an excellent choice for those who enjoy country settings rather than beach resorts, though it opens for only a very limited period in the peak summer months. The views from here across the west coast are splendid, and in spring the woods are carpeted in anemones and cyclamens. The hotel is operated by the Astir group (which also runs the deluxe Grand Hotel Astir Palace in Rhodes Town). Grade A.

Ayios Nikolaos Fountoukli church is renowned for its frescos

♦♦♦
SIMI
about 15 miles (24km) north of Rhodes island

The small, friendly island of Simi, which lies between two Turkish peninsulas, is an increasingly popular place for an interesting day's excursion from Rhodes – it is the second nearest of the Dodecanese after Khálki. It is also becoming more popular as a holiday destination in its own right, although a shortage of accommodation is a problem many would-be visitors encounter. At first sight the island appears unoccupied and barren, apart from a few pine forests; but as you approach the long harbour you discover a large, 19th-century Greek island town, preserved in almost perfect detail. The little port of **Yialós** is breathtaking, with neoclassical houses in ochre and pastel shades in tiers on the rocky hillsides. Many were abandoned or bombed in World War II, but they are now being restored from their state of faded glory. Conservation is a keyword on the island: no high-rise concrete monstrosities here! There is a small beach at the port, and the rock swimming and sunbathing are good; there is also windsurfing and waterskiing.

Fresh water supplies for washing can be a problem on Simi, and in the high season you should be prepared for occasional water rationing. The village is also steeply stepped, making it unsuitable for the elderly or those with walking difficulties. As an example, there are about 500 steps from

RESORTS

SÍMI

Khondrós

Nímos

Ákra
Koutsoumbas

Embório

Ákra
Filonikos

Moní
Roukouniotis

Yialós
Sími

Pédhion
Chorio

Ayiou Vasilíou

Vígla
620m

Órmos
Ayiou Vasilíou

Órmos
Nanóu

Ákra
Áyios Nikólaos

Limín
Panormítis

Marathoúnda

Panormítis

Moní Taxiarkhis
Michael

Ákra Pátos

270m

0 1 2 3km
0   1   2miles

Sésklion

What to See and Do

Motorcycles and cars can be
hired for sightseeing, but there
is only one roughly hewn main
road, more suitable for donkeys
than vehicles. However, the
island now boasts an air-
conditioned coach to take you in
style through the interior to
**Moní (monastery of) Taxiarchis
Michael** at Panormítis – a vast,
white edifice in a lovely
horseshoe bay and a place of
pilgrimage for Greeks
worldwide. The Archangel
Michael is the island's patron
saint and protector of sailors.
The church is rich with gold and
silver offerings from grateful
mariners, and there is a small
museum in the peaceful
courtyard. Sometimes there is a
stop at another small monastery
on the way, and you can return
by boat after relaxing on the
beach at Marathoúnda.
Daily excursions are available
by caïque to various bays
around the island, all offering
sheltered shingle or pebble
beaches, with excellent
swimming and snorkelling in
crystal clear waters.
If you are interested in walking,
apart from the endless
exploration of the town and
nearby fertile valley, there are
guided walks over the island by
a resident Englishman. They
start at about 07.00hrs to escape
the main heat of the sun, and
last two to five hours,
depending on the route, with
various stops for rest and
looking at the interesting
aspects of the island. These
walks normally finish by joining
up with an excursion boat for a
barbecue lunch.

the harbour to the museum in
the upper town, and 650 steps to
the very top of the town. Those
seeking a relaxing, peaceful
holiday should also be warned
that between the hours of 11.00
and 16.00 the port becomes
very crowded with day trippers
from Rhodes.
The harbour area is the social
centre of the island, where most
of the shops, tavernas and cafés
are located. Down on the other
side of Chorio – the upper
village – a road leads through a
valley to **Pédhion**, a hamlet of
fishermen's cottages, which now
has a hotel on the sandy shore,
several tavernas, and an
'ouzerie' where you can sample
a Nun's Bikini cocktail made
from the unusual local cactus
flower liqueur!
Simi is especially attractive at
Easter, when special cheese
pies and biscuits are baked. On
Easter Saturday night fireworks
fill the air in celebration of the
great festival.

Simi's dazzling palette of colours

Accommodation

Accommodation on Simi is expensive and difficult to obtain, especially if you are looking for a single night's stay — owners usually insist on a minimum of two or three days' room occupation. The general standard of accommodation is fairly basic.

Hotel Aliki, Yialós (tel: 71665). Arguably the best hotel on the island, this large, neoclassical mansion, situated on the sea front, has been tastefully converted to a small hotel, with 15 rooms of varying sizes, furnished to a high standard. On the ground floor there is an elegant bar and breakfast room, and there is also a roof-garden with magnificent views of the bay of Simi. It is possible to swim and snorkel off the rocks

RESORTS

directly in front of the hotel, and it is only five minutes' walk to the central harbour area. The owner provides a warm and welcoming atmosphere. Grade A.

Chorio Hotel, Chorio (tel: 71800). This recently-built bed and breakfast hotel is situated at the end of the row of windmills above the port. The hotel is in true Simi style, only two storeys high and painted a wonderful sky blue. The rooms have been well furnished, with great attention to detail. Nine have private balconies, and there are several quiet terraces and patios where guests can sit and enjoy peace, sunshine and a drink from the bar. There is also a comfortable lounge and a pretty dining room. The hotel is only minutes away from Chorio's lively tavernas, and right next to the village bus stop, with buses going to both Pédhion Bay and the harbour area. Grade B.

Hotel Grace, Yialós (tel: 71415). This small, family-run bed and breakfast hotel is situated in a quiet position about five minutes' walk from Yialós' tavernas and shops. Yiannis, the owner, has recently added a new wing, with three rooms and two studios, all of which share a beautiful terrace with glorious views over the harbour. The rooms all have refrigerators and private bathrooms with solar water heating. There is a telephone in reception for guests' use, and breakfast is served under a leafy vine on the terrace. The rooms are all nicely furnished, and the hotel has been built to a very high standard. Grade B.

Kokona Hotel, Yialós (tel: 71451). This spotless, family-run bed and breakfast hotel stands on the harbour level, two minutes' walk from the quayside yet in one of the quietest spots in Simi's harbour village. Fotis, the owner, is a carpenter by trade, and his skills are apparent in the attractive bedrooms, with lovely pinewood fixtures and furnishings. Each room has a telephone, fan, and private bathroom with hot water. Most have either balcony or terrace. Kokona, Fotis' wife, serves breakfast on the vine-covered terrace outside the hotel, and in the basement there is a small bar. Grade B.

Pedi Beach Hotel, Pédhion (tel: 71276). The hotel is situated at Pédhion Beach, about 40 minutes' walk from Simi harbour. All the rooms have balconies or terraces, and most face the sea. The situation is quiet, with a beautiful outlook over the countryside or the sea. A regular bus service or a short journey by taxi takes you to either Chorio or Simi harbour, for a wider choice of restaurants, bars and shopping. Grade B.

Restaurants and Entertainment

For eating out, there are many tavernas around the harbour-front, and also in the upper town of Chorio: fresh fish and locally caught shrimps are a speciality. At weekends there are usually impromptu bouzouki evenings in Chorio and Pédhion, but every night the tavernas, cafés and bars can become quite lively. Well away from the port are two discothèques.

Fishermen's chapel at Stegna

◆◆
STEGNA
east coast

Though not exactly the prettiest resort on Rhodes, Stegna is certainly one of the least spoiled and least commercialised, as yet virtually undiscovered by the masses. Set on the side of an attractive bay, the village straggles along the seashore, and includes several fishermen's shacks and a couple of unpretentious tavernas – an ideal spot for those who enjoy simple pleasures without any frills. As for the beach, there is a fine, shingle, sandy foreshore giving way to pebbles; although not really equipped for visitors, it does have a few beach umbrellas and windsurfing boards for hire, and there are also beach showers. The resort is reached from the village of Arkhángelos via a winding, tortuous road complete with hairpin bends, so care needs to be taken, whether you are driving or on foot.

◆◆
THEOLÓGOS
west coast, about 14 miles (22km) from Rhodes Town

The little village of Theológos is an uncommercialised retreat, in a rural setting, with a pebble beach and few facilities apart from a handful of tavernas, a mini-market, and a village baker. It is popular with those looking for a quiet, away-from-it-all stay, but as bus services are limited, a rented car is recommended if you want to get out and about.

Note that the village is only three miles (5km) from the airport, so some aircraft noise can be experienced, though this is not usually a problem.

RESORTS

Accommodation

Hotel Doreta Beach (tel: 41441).
This comfortable hotel has been
a favourite with British visitors
for many years. It stands in
attractive gardens stretching
down to the beach, about a mile
(2km) from the village centre.
The hotel is cool and spacious
inside, and imaginative use of
local stonework gives the décor
a typical Greek quality.
Facilities include a split-level
lounge and bar, two lifts, a
hairdresser, two shops, a
supermarket, large swimming-
pool with sun terrace, poolside
snack bar/taverna, and a
children's club run by a
supervisor. For toddlers there is
also a paddling pool and a
playground with a safe, sandy
base; early dinners are
available along with a special
menu; and babysitting can be
arranged on request. Grade A.

Hotel Meliton (tel: 41666). In a
peaceful setting on the outskirts
of Theológos – about 15 minutes'
walk from the beach and 20
minutes' from shops and
tavernas in the centre of the
resort – the Meliton was built to
a standard much higher than is
normally expected of its
C-grade rating. Facilities
include a comfortable lounge
bar and attractive gardens
which contain a pool and tennis
courts, with equipment available
for hire.

Entertainment

The **Lemon Tree** bar along the
road from the Hotel Doreta
Beach is popular with hotel
guests and other visitors to the
resort.

Moorish arch at Thermai Kallithéa

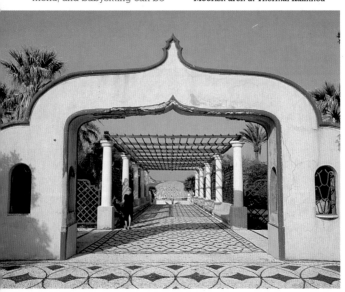

◆◆◆
THERMAI KALLITHÉA
(Kalithea)
about 2½ miles (4km) south of Rhodes Town
Thermai Kallithéa was built in the 1920s by the Italians as a spa. It enjoyed considerable popularity with visitors anxious to take what they believed were the healing waters, said to be beneficial in the treatment of rheumatism, arthritis, diabetes and kidney diseases. Now the attractive domed pavilions with pink marbled pillars and Moorish archways stand abandoned. But although its life as a health spa is over, Kalithea has a new lease of life as a holiday resort catering to sun-worshippers, with a small development growing up around the nearby small, sheltered cove. Here you will find a few tavernas and a small but pleasant shingle beach, with rocky coves. There is also a lido beneath the palm trees with sun-loungers and a café.

Accommodation
Eden Roc Hotel (tel: 23851). Located along the bay of Kalithea, in the direction of Falirakion, the Eden Roc fronts a rocky stretch of beach. It offers waterskiing, bicycling, windsurfing, two large tennis courts, and a sauna. Grade A.
Paradise Hotel (tel: 29220). One of Rhodes' finest hotels of its class, with a high standard of comfort and excellent facilities, the 645-room Paradise enjoys an attractive setting near Kalithea, with steps leading down from the sun terrace to the sheltered sand and shingle cove below.

Among its amenities are a large swimming-pool with sun terraces and gardens, together with beach and poolside bars; air-conditioning throughout in high season; two bars and lounges; discothèque and nightclub; and facilities for tennis, windsurfing, waterskiing, table tennis and mini-golf. For youngsters there is a children's pool, early suppers, and high chairs and cots on request. Grade A.
Sunwing Hotel (tel: 28600). Facilities here range from a large restaurant overlooking the swimming-pool and sea to a beach taverna, cocktail bar, and grill terrace with dancing, shows and entertainment. Sports facilities include two tennis courts, mini-golf and volley ball. Grade A.

Restaurant
Home-made Greek dishes are a speciality of the restaurant/bar **Koskinou House**.

◆◆
TRIÁNDA
west coast
Triánda (or sometimes Trianta in tour operators' brochures) is rapidly developing as a resort, not least because of its convenient location not far from Rhodes Town and because it is on the doorstep of one of the most fascinating ancient sites on the island – Ialyssos. The resort is situated on the main route into Rhodes Town from the airport. The fact that it is quite close to the airport, means that it suffers from occasional aircraft noise. Other disadvantages are that the sea here tends to be less calm than at other resorts along

this coast, and that the beaches tend to shelve quite steeply, making it not the best choice for those with young children. That said, the grey sand and shingle beach – about fifteen minutes' walk from the resort centre – is very popular in the high season, especially with windsurfers and sailors. Pedaloes are available for rent and some of the hotels offer sports facilities.

First settled by Minoans from Crete in the 16th century BC, Triánda was inundated by tidal waves during the following century when the volcanic island of Santorini, near Crete, erupted. It is said that the name, meaning 'thirty', derives from the establishment here of that number of summer villas belonging to the Knights of St John. Today's visitors can enjoy a resort that retains a fair degree of village atmosphere, with a pleasant square containing bars, tavernas and cafés that are popular gathering places for visitors and locals.

If you decide to venture away from the beach for a while you can explore the site of the ancient city of **Ialyssos**, with its 3rd-century temple, ruined castle, restored monastery and centuries-old Doric fountain (page 55). The church in Triánda, dedicated to the Assumption of the Holy Mary, has a splendidly carved 18th-century screen.

Accommodation

Accommodation in Triánda is mixed, with hotels of varying standards and also self-catering apartments and studios. The accommodation tends to be spread out over quite an extensive area, with some establishments in isolated positions away from the village.

Blue Horizon Hotel (tel: (93481). A recently built hotel with 221 rooms, bungalows and suites, each with terrace or balcony, bathroom, telephone and radio, the Blue Horizon is located on a stretch of shingle beach about ten minutes from the resort centre. The hotel's reception area is attractively designed and filled with tropical plants, and there is a large, pleasant dining room, snack bar, swimming-pool, children's pool and playground, bar and taverna. Grade A.

Filerimos Hotel (tel: 29510). Located about ten minutes' walk from the beach and 15 minutes from the centre of Triánda, the Filerimos is part of a complex that also includes apartment accommodation. Facilities, shared by all guests, include two swimming-pools set in sun terraces, a poolside snack bar, two lounges, a supermarket and a gift shop. The hotel's taverna offers a choice of local and international dishes, while regular Greek evenings are a popular feature, as is dancing to records in one of the hotel's lounge bars. Grade A.

Hotel Golden Beach (tel: 92411). Superbly located on a private stretch of pebble beach, with views of the sea from the front and of mountains from the rear, the Golden Beach is a pleasant, well maintained hotel that is popular with families and fully justifies its A-grade classification. There are 196 twin-bedded rooms and 10

Doric temple ruins, Ialyssos

singles, all with air-conditioning, balconies and private facilities, and there are also 55 self-catering apartments.
The Olympic-sized swimming-pool is complemented by a separate, freshwater children's pool, both are set in attractive gardens. There is also a restaurant, a snack bar, a piano bar and a nightclub offering open-air dancing.
Hotel Sunflower (tel: 93893). Popular with German, Dutch and English visitors, this is an impressive 87-room hotel that offers a large, oblong swimming-pool and beautiful gardens with plenty of sunbeds, tables and chairs.
The small dining room offers an international menu, with buffet breakfasts, and there are early meals for children. On the negative side, there is a potentially dangerous three-sided lift, and no depth marking in the swimming-pool making careful supervision of children necessary. Grade A.

Restaurants and Entertainment
For evening entertainment there are several local restaurants serving Greek cuisine and there is also a popular disco for the young-at-heart. One of the most unusual café/bars is created from an old windmill sitting right by the beach and called, not surprisingly, the **Windmill**. The nearby **Trata** taverna specialises in fresh fish.

RESORTS

◆◆
TSAMBIKA

east coast, about 18 miles (30km) from Rhodes Town

This is a beautiful bay bordered by a long, sandy beach, approached down a steep access road. Some guide books describe the place as being uncrowded and undiscovered, but in fact it is extremely popular in high summer, attracting people staying in other parts of the island, who come here in their droves by coach, rented cars and even boats. Beach and watersports lovers, however, are well catered for, with rafts, pedaloes, speedboats, umbrellas and sunbeds all available for rent, and the adventurous can even try parascending here. **Vidal's Saloon**, a small but popular beach taverna, has a shower point on the edge of its patio. Away from the beach, a turning off the Tsambika Beach road leads to a white, Byzantine monastery surrounded by stone walls. Being set close to the mountain top, it affords splendid views. On 8 September each year, women wishing to conceive climb the steep approach on foot and pray that they may give birth.

◆◆◆
YENNÁDHION (Gennadi)

southeast coast

On such a popular island as Rhodes, it is surprising that until quite recently Yennádhion had escaped the attention of most holiday companies, although this is changing rapidly, with studios and apartments beginning to spring up like mushrooms.

Orange trees – a refreshing sight

Surrounded by delightful countryside and situated on an extensive bay, this area enjoys some of the best beaches on the island, though Yennádhion beach itself is of sand and shingle. Numerous tracks lead down from the road to the beach, with its dunes and crystal clear sea, and also to numerous seafood tavernas found on this pretty coastline. Prices as well as time have tended to stand still here – you will find it cheaper than most other areas of Rhodes. The nightlife is limited in the extreme, and there are no discos, but for those opting for self-catering accommodation, there are a few mini-markets, and a post office.

PEACE AND QUIET

Wildlife and Countryside on Rhodes
by Paul Sterry

Although it is extremely popular as a tourist destination, most of the associated development on Rhodes has been concentrated in a few areas, largely along the coast and in the north of the island. Happily, much of the interior and southern half remains unspoiled.

For such a comparatively small island, Rhodes boasts a wide range of habitats. The coastline is superb, with dramatic cliffs, isolated coves and deserted and windswept beaches. Inland there are still areas of natural woodland, sadly depleted by recent fires, together with maquis and phrygana vegetation – habitats typical of many Mediterranean islands. Much of the remaining land is under cultivation, but because the farming is not intensive, the small fields still support a surprising range of wildlife. Although there is wildlife interest throughout the year, spring is undoubtedly the best season to visit Rhodes. Migrant birds are newly arrived and flowers bloom everywhere.

The Coast

The seas and coast which surround Rhodes are perhaps its crowning glory: there are stunning sea cliffs and beautiful sandy beaches, many of which – especially on the west coast – are virtually deserted. The seas are full of marine life – food for a typical range of Mediterranean sea birds – while on land, the coast is home to colourful maritime plants.

The west coast of Rhodes in particular is constantly buffeted by onshore winds and consequently is noticeably cooler than the east side of the island. From about 11.00hrs onwards the winds pick up and oceanic birds such as Cory's shearwaters and Manx shearwaters often pass surprisingly close to shore. Both species are masters of the seas and their gliding flight, on outstretched wings, is seemingly effortless. They fly in long lines of birds, close to the water, and characteristically twist and turn to make the most of the sea breezes.

Snorkelling in the clear, blue waters reveals a wealth of life unseen from land. Because the Mediterranean has an extremely small tidal range, rock pools are seldom exposed, and marine creatures such as sea urchins, starfish and sea anemones have to be viewed from under water. Some marine life does get washed ashore after strong winds, however, and sea balls – compacted balls of sea grass – are often conspicuous. For those who do not wish to go snorkelling or scuba diving, there is an excellent marine aquarium in Rhodes town.

The flowers of the coast are at their best in spring and early summer. Along the cliffs, look for hottentot fig – an introduction from southern Africa – while shingle beaches and sand dunes may have species such as yellow-horned poppy and purple spurge, together with the

A bee-eater surveys the scene

ubiquitous agave or century plant. When in flower, the plants of the sand dunes are visited by colourful butterflies, including clouded yellows and painted ladies, as well as day-flying hummingbird hawk moths.

Agricultural Land

The farming methods on Rhodes are generally traditional and small scale, and the landscape has probably changed little over the last hundred years. Small fields, surrounded by stone walls built from rubble removed from the soil, are typical, as are olive groves and orchards of citrus fruits. The tall spires of funereal cypress trees dot the landscape and a surprising range of wildlife flourishes alongside the crops.

One of the pleasures of walking on Rhodes is the delightful small fields, full of colourful flowers in spring. A wide range of arable 'weeds' can be found among the cereal crops and more especially in fallow fields. Star thistles – plants with typical thistle flowers but incredibly spiny stems and leaves – grape hyacinths, anemones and poppies appear, and even in the height of summer, field eryngo – another very spiny plant – St John's worts, mulleins and mallows can be found. The flowers are visited by butterflies such as the elegant scarce swallowtail, while on the ground, grasshoppers and crickets scurry for cover.

Farm buildings and overgrown gardens sometimes harbour interesting birds and insects. The sound of cicadas is deafening during the height of summer, many of their number falling victim to praying mantids which lurk among the foliage. Serins – wild relatives of the canary – are less intrusive, singing their jingling song from the tops of trees.

Maquis

Originally, much of Rhodes would have been cloaked in evergreen oaks and pines, with a rich understorey of flowers appearing in glades and rides. Over the centuries, the trees were gradually cleared for timber, firewood and to create agricultural land. In many areas, the forests never fully regenerated, partly due to the actions of grazing animals. However, a form of natural vegetation – maquis – colonised some areas, characterised by a wide range of colourful and aromatic plants.

On Rhodes, maquis vegetation is typical of many of the mountain roads, such as that between Afándou (on the east coast) and Psínthos. Kermes oak, whose leaves resemble miniature holly leaves, and mastic trees are prominent and there is usually a dense understorey of tree heathers, cistuses, rosemary, juniper, rock roses and thorn of Christ. Many of the plants are spiny or have leaves which are waxy or aromatic; this discourages grazing animals and helps reduce water loss.

During the long, dry summer many Mediterranean snails go into a dormant state known as aestivation. They gather together in clusters, sometimes of several dozen individuals, on plant stems. The egg cases of praying mantids are also attached to stems and have an extremely hard texture.

Phrygana

Phrygana vegetation is typical of dry, stony land which in the past was probably covered by open, stunted woodland. This habitat is characterised by low-growing plants and shrubs, some of which are spiny and form dense, compact cushions. In addition to the more persistent species such as asphodels, hypericums, heathers and vetches, spring sees the appearance of grape hyacinths, French lavenders, spurges and cistuses.

One of the glories of a spring visit to Rhodes is the discovery of numerous orchids, both in phrygana and in maquis habitats. Several members of the bee orchid family are widespread. More showy in appearance are butterfly orchids, tongue orchids, bug orchids and giant orchids, the latter a particularly early flowering species. You are likely to come across them almost anywhere, but verges and abandoned fields can be particularly good. Orchids can be extraordinarily difficult to spot, even giant orchids, which regularly grow to three feet (one metre) tall, but once you have 'got your eye in' more and more will swim into view.

Birds of the Fields

Typical birds of agricultural land include little owls and crested larks, the latter species often rather inconspicuous as its plumage blends in with the dusty soil. Look for little owls perched on fence posts or overhanging branches. They will follow your movements with their eyes, and have the disconcerting ability to turn their heads almost through 180 degrees in any direction, including upside-down, without having to move their bodies. Corn buntings, whose song is supposed to resemble jingling keys, are widespread and sing from exposed perches, while Sardinian warblers can be seen or heard wherever there is dense cover. In the summer months, black-headed buntings perch on overhead wires and on branches.

In spring and autumn, migrant birds stop off to feed. Short-toed larks, black redstarts, tawny pipits and the occasional red-throated pipit can also be found feeding in bare fields. Birds of prey, including harriers and kestrels, quarter the fields in search of insects and small mammals, while bee-eaters and rollers perch on wires to scan the surrounding land for prey.

PEACE AND QUIET

Forests and Mountains

With the exception of Mount Atáviros, most of the mountains on Rhodes are, to some extent, wooded. The forests comprise mainly pines, with some evergreen oaks, and often develop a rich understorey of maquis vegetation. Sadly, in recent years there have been extensive fires, many started deliberately, which have not only reduced the area of forests but also severely depleted the range of wildlife they support. Under the open canopy of many undisturbed pine woodlands, a dense layer of maquis plants such as tree heathers, junipers, cistuses and spurges can be found. The air is full of aromatic scents from the low-growing plants and the pines.

Mount Atáviros lies on the west side of Rhodes and rises to 4,000 feet (1,215m) above sea-level. A dramatic gorge is carved into the western side of its bare limestone slopes, and this can be seen from the road. Crag martins are often seen around the mountain. These aerobatic brown birds can be told from other martins and swallows by the wedge-shaped tail with its row of small, white blobs. Their close relative, the sand martin, has white underparts with a brown breast band.

Visitors should also look for jackdaws and ravens, the latter being easily told by their large size, jet-black plumage, wedge-shaped tail in flight and loud 'cronking' call. It is worthwhile watching ravens on the wing, not only for their amazing aerobatic displays, but also because they mob birds of prey that intrude into their territories. Peregrines are the most usual species to be seen, but during spring and autumn migration periods, it is worth checking each raptor you see carefully because many other species pass through on passage.

The Líndhos Peninsula

Set on the east side of Rhodes, this is the driest, hottest part of the island. Near the town of Líndhos are dramatic sea cliffs and the famous acropolis. Here the cliffs drop sheer away to the azure waters of the Mediterranean. Before long, visitors will see crag martins feeding in small parties on the wing, hunting for insects close to the cliff face. They are sometimes seen in the company of swifts and the occasional alpine swift – the latter species has a white rump and throat and is considerably larger than its more common relative. In spring, blue rock thrushes sing their attractive song from rocky promontories along the cliff edge. Views stretch inland across large areas of phrygana habitat, characterised by low-growing plants and stony ground.

Cape Prasonísi

Cape Prasonísi lies at the southern tip of Rhodes and is a largely uninhabited and unspoilt region. The cape itself is connected to the mainland of Rhodes by a tombolo – a sand bar, covered only by the highest of tides – and the whole area is covered in excellent phrygana vegetation.

*Jersey tiger moths in the Valley of
the Butterflies, Petaloudhes*

As you approach the cape from
the main road, you drive across
a flat, agricultural plain. The
fields here are excellent for
arable 'weeds' in the spring,
and are very likely to contain
both migrant and resident birds.
Larks, pipits and wheatears
feed on the ground, while
bee-eaters perch on wires and
birds of prey quarter the
ground in search of insects and
lizards.

Having reached the sand
tombolo, it is best to park before
you reach the beach itself
because the sand is extremely
soft in places. The seas to the
west of the beach are beloved
of windsurfers. During periods
of strong, onshore winds,
seabirds also make use of the
sea breezes, sometimes coming
surprisingly close to shore.
The phrygana vegetation which
covers much of the cape is
perhaps the best example of
this habitat on the island. In
spring, the dwarfed and
flattened plants become
studded with colourful flowers;
cistuses, rosemary, thyme and
spiny vetches are common.

The Valley of the Butterflies

The Valley of the Butterflies at
Petaloudhes is world famous
and attracts large numbers of
tourists each year. Although the
name is rather misleading – the
'butterflies' are in fact Jersey

tiger moths – the name has stuck and thousands of people visit the site each year to witness the mass concentration of these insects during the hot summer months.

From the roadside car park, visitors pay to enter the site and then follow the streamside walk up the valley. The route is lined with oriental plane trees in which you may see birds such as robins, spotted flycatchers and wrens. There are fish in the deep pools and freshwater crabs scurry along the water's edge. Further up the valley, the crabs catch the moths, and their discarded wings can be seen beside the stream.

Because of the shade and humidity provided by the stream and the woodland, maidenhair fern flourishes beside the water. It is precisely these same environmental conditions, together with the supply of resin from the plane trees, that attract the Jersey tiger moths. Damp rock faces, tree trunks and branches and streamside boulders are covered with these attractive insects, which spend the dry summer months in the valley, departing only when the autumn rains arrive.

Sadly, tourism is having a detrimental effect on the moths: despite notices requesting visitors not to interfere with them, they are constantly disturbed and as a consequence fewer and fewer are seen each year. Hopefully, stricter enforcement of the notice may halt their decline.

If you continue up the valley past the main concentrations of moths, the woodland gradually becomes less disturbed. Having crossed a road, the stream eventually dries up and as soon as the water disappears, so do the moths. The path eventually leads out of the valley and on to an old monastery. From here, good views can be had down the valley and visitors should look out for peregrines and ravens overhead.

The Valley of the Butterflies lies west of Maritsá, off the road from Kalamón to Psínthos.

Kamiros Skala Castle

The Kastellos at Kamiros Skala (see page 64) is situated on the northwest coast near Kritinía and is marked as an ancient monument on most maps of the island. In addition to its historic interest, the castle is surrounded by excellent woodland and maquis and there are inspiring views along the coast. Visitors should be aware, however, of military restrictions which apply to parts of the surrounding land and should take due note of the 'No Photography' signs.

The castle is reached along a stony path from the main coast road. The cliffs below the site are very steep and are the haunt of birds such as blue rock thrushes, crag martins, ravens and the occasional peregrine. However, it is the woodland and maquis which border the castle that are perhaps of more interest to the visiting naturalist. In spring, the flowers are colourful and varied. Tree heathers, brooms, juniper and cistuses are most conspicuous, but there are several species of orchids which can also be found by careful searching: giant orchid, sombre bee orchid and late spider orchid are among the most widespread. There are interesting plants to be found later in the season, one of the highlights being the beautiful flowers of caper, which can be found growing in the woods close to the ruins.

The Bay of Afándou

The sweeping Bay of Afándou (Órmos Afándou) lies south of Rhodes Town on the northeast coast between Cape (Ákra) Ladhikó and Cape Vayia. Although the southern parts of the bay are beginning to be developed for tourism, most of the shoreline is unspoilt and traditional farming and cultivation continues inland. The beach has maritime flowers, sea birds can be seen offshore, and

Purple spurge on a shingle beach

inland, migrant and resident birds can be seen in olive groves and fields which are full of colourful flowers in spring. The beach which fringes the Bay of Afándou is surprisingly varied, with areas of sand, but also with shingle and boulders, which discourage many people. Spurges, yellow-horned poppies and rock samphire can be found growing above the tideline and Kentish plovers grace the shoreline. These delightful little waders – grey on top and bright white below – are particularly attracted to areas of the bay where streams, which are dry for most of the year, come down to the beach. Some of the inland fields are bordered with sandy banks, which attract bee-eaters. These colourful and aerobatic birds excavate burrows in the banks in which to nest, and their excited, bubbling calls are a familiar sound around the fields.

Their bright colours – vivid green, red ochre, yellow and black – make them exciting birds to spot. Bee-eaters specialise in catching insects on the wing and their graceful flight looks seemingly effortless as they glide and circle overhead.

The Southwest Coast

The southwest coast of Rhodes is fringed by an immense sandy beach. Because it is a long way from the centres of tourism and the prevailing onshore winds make the seas rough for much of the time, it is largely unexplored and undeveloped. Here, visitors can explore the beaches in isolation and find a wide range of wildlife, not only along the shoreline but also in the juniper scrub and maquis which lies inland.

A rough road (linking Apolakkiá with Kattavía) runs parallel with the beach for most of its length but there are few stopping places and access to the shore is by the occasional gravel track.

Bird Migration

Many of the birds commonly found breeding in northern Europe during the summer months are not resident throughout the year but fly south each autumn to escape the winter and find better feeding. Some spend the winter around the Mediterranean but many fly further south to Africa. To avoid flying directly over the Mediterranean, millions of birds travel around the sea's eastern coast in spring and trickle along its northern shoreline, taking the reverse route each autumn.

Rhodes lying only a short distance from the Turkish coast, it is not surprising that large numbers pass through on spring and autumn migration and a good range of species can be found during these periods. These include both summer breeding visitors to Rhodes and species *en route* to more northerly latitudes.

Spring migration begins in March and continues until May. Among the first birds to arrive are the martins – both house martins and sand martins will be seen – and swallows. Among the parties of swallows there are also likely to be the less widespread red-rumped swallows, which frequently associate with them. The latter species can be easily distinguished by its pale buffish-red rump and collar. Even on migration, birds tend to rest and feed in the habitats to which they are most suited. Thus, wheatears, larks and pipits can be found in arable fields and on bare ground, while warblers and flycatchers prefer scrub vegetation with plenty of cover.

Among the larger birds, a wide range of birds of prey also migrate through the region – harriers, honey buzzards, lesser kestrels and the occasional red-footed falcon. They appear in both spring and autumn, which is also the case with rollers and bee-eaters. These two are without doubt the most colourful species to be seen on Rhodes and, fortunately, their habit of perching on wires and dead branches makes them easy to see.

FOOD AND DRINK

Sizzling meat in a psistaria

FOOD AND DRINK

Because of the popularity of Rhodes among the Scandinavians and British, authentic, traditional Greek cuisine is becoming less important in the island's major holiday resorts. Instead, most tourist hotels and restaurants serve 'international' fare to please foreign tastes. Chicken, lamb chops, sausage-egg-and-chips and the like feature large, and there are often special children's menus. However, many establishments also offer Greek cuisine as an alternative. and this is often of a high standard.

Restaurants and tavernas abound throughout the island, most of them representing reasonable value, although standards of service vary wildly. A smart appearance is by no means a good indication of

quality – in fact, the more basic tavernas are often the best, especially if they are frequented by the locals. Even if you cannot understand the menu, you can always go into the kitchen and make a choice from the dishes you see being prepared. A *psistaria* specialises in meats grilled over charcoal, and, in resorts, may double as a fast food outlet serving pizzas, toasted sandwiches and hamburgers. In Rhodes Town you will also find small shops selling Greek fast food. Fish *(psari)* such as lobster, crayfish, shrimps, squid and swordfish, seem reasonably priced to many visitors, although it is no longer the staple food of the locals: pollution and plundering of the seas have made prices rise. Although menus are often limited in

FOOD AND DRINK

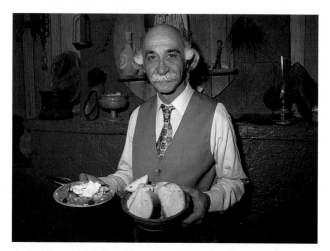

choice, there is usually lamb, pork and chicken on offer. Those unaccustomed to Greek food may find it a little greasy, and for some reason the islanders seem to prefer their meals served warm rather than hot. Eating establishments are price controlled according to category, and though the service charge is included in the bill, it is customary to leave a little extra for the waiter.

Greek Cuisine

Menus are often in Greek, English, French, German and Swedish (with some bizarre translations). They will offer a limited choice that includes *mezedes* (hors d'oeuvres) and *tis oras* (meat and fish fried or grilled to order). What is on the menu will not necessarily be available – it is only a rough guide. The waiter will tell you what is 'on'.

Since the idea of courses is foreign to Greek cuisine,

Service with a smile in a taverna

starters, main dishes and salads often arrive together. The best thing is to order a selection of *mezedes* and salads to share among your party. The most interesting *mezedes* are *tzatziki* (yoghurt, garlic and cucumber dip); *melitzanosalata* (aubergine dip); courgettes or aubergines fried in batter; white haricot beans in vinaigrette sauce; *tiropitakia* or *spanakopites* (small cheese and spinach pies); *saganaki* (fried cheese); *oktapóthi* (octopus); *mavromatika* (black-eyed peas); and *dolmadakia* (vine leaves stuffed with meat or rice). Other typical *mezedes* are *garides* (shrimps), *feta* (white goat's cheese), *taramosalata* (pâté of smoked fish roe) and *bourekakia* (small meat pies). The so-called Greek salad (*horiatiki* to the Greeks) is served with everything. It consists of tomato and cucumber wedges, onion rings and red and green peppers, topped with *feta* and olives and sprinkled with oregano. Olive oil is usually added, but you could ask for it to be omitted. A simple tomato and cucumber salad is *angour domata*.

Meat Dishes

Shish kebab *(souvlákia)* and chops *(brizoles)* are usually reliable choices. The best *souvláki* is made from lamb *(arnisio)*, but it is not often available. Nowadays these skewers of grilled meat, tomato, peppers and onions are often made with pork. The small lamb cutlets called *paidhákia* are usually very tasty, as is roast lamb *(arni psito)* and roast kid *(katsiki)*, when obtainable. *Kefthedes* (meatballs), *biftekia* (a type of hamburger), and the spicy sausages called *loukanika* are usually good and cheap, although minced meat is the most common source of stomach problems in Rhodes as elsewhere, so it is important that such items are freshly made and thoroughly cooked. Restaurants with a fast turnover, and frequented by locals, are likely to be safe.

Another meat-based main course dish the visitor to Rhodes is likely to encounter is moussaka, a pie authentically made from aubergines and minced meat (preferably lamb, now often beef) topped with a custardy cheese sauce and baked. Among the many other tasty main courses found in tavernas are *pastitsio* (macaroni with minced meat and béchamel sauce), *gemista*

(either tomatoes or green peppers stuffed with meat or rice), *yiouvarelákia* (stewed meat balls with rice), *souzoukákia* (meat balls with tomato sauce and garlic), *stifado* (meat with onions), *kokoretsi* (skewers of liver and kidneys) and *pastitsada* (tomato stew).

Fish

Coastal tavernas in Rhodes and many establishment in Rhodes Town, especially the medieval quarter, also offer fish and shellfish. *Kalamarákia* (fried baby squid) are widely available in summer, but the choice fish, such as red mullet *(barbounia)* and sea bream *(fangri)* are much less common and much more expensive. Among the fish and seafood dishes fairly widely available are *astakós* (lobster), *kavouri* (crab), *stridia* (oysters), *midia* (clams), *lithrinia* (bass), *glossa* (sole) and *marídes* (whitebait). *Youvetsi* is a shrimp casserole. Less pricey but equally tasty are *xifhias*, grilled pieces of swordfish served on skewers with onions, tomatoes and bay leaves. The price of fish is quoted by the kilo, and the standard procedure is to 'go to the glass' (which may mean a tank or refrigerator) and choose your own.

Desserts

Restaurants catering for tourists may serve a limited choice of desserts, but after a meal most Greeks prefer to go to a *zaharoplastion* (pâtisserie), where sticky, sweet confections are served with a glass of water, or may be taken out in a box. Fruit is often the most delicious

FOOD AND DRINK

dessert. Watermelon *(karpouzi)*, and *peponi* (a melon with a somewhat unusual taste) are the standard summer fruit, along with peaches, oranges, figs and seedless grapes. You will also find ice cream *(pagotó)*, often home-made and usually creamy and very good. Yoghurt with honey is a simple and delicious finish to a meal. Other desserts include *pastes* (very sweet cakes with cream), *baklavá* (syrup cake with nuts), *loukoumádes* (fritters with honey or syrup), and *kataifi* (shredded wheat soaked in honey). One of Rhodes' specialities is *rizogalo*, cold rice pudding flavoured with lemon and cinnamon. You can usually find it in Rhodes Town at a *galaktopolio*, a dairy counter selling items such as yoghurt, milk, butter and pastries.

Snacks

Traditional snacks are one of the delights of Greek cuisine, although they are being increasingly replaced by international favourites such as toasted sandwiches *(tost)*, and pizzas. However, small kebabs *(souvlákia)* can sometimes be found in Rhodes, especially in Rhodes Town, and cheese pies *(tiropites)* can almost always be found at the baker's. Another popular snack is *yiro* (doner kebab) served in pitta bread with garnish.

Drinks

Wine *(krasi)* is commonly drunk on Rhodes. White is *aspro krasi*, red is *mavro krasi*, and both leave that unique Greek aftertaste which you either love or hate. Acceptable local wines include Líndhos Blanc Sec and Grand Maître (both white) and Chevalier de Rhodes, a red wine.

Retsina, a wine flavoured with pine resin, which comes from mainland Greece, should be served chilled and is available from bottles or from barrels. Un-resinated Demesticha is available as white or red, and is inexpensive.

Greek brandy *(conyak)* can be dreadful or excellent; cheaper brands tend to be rather sweet, while the well-known brands (usually more reliable) are Botrys, Metaxa and Cambas, of which different qualities are produced. But imported spirits and drinks such as whisky, gin and vermouth are often no more expensive than locally produced equivalents, thanks to Rhodes' duty-free status.

Beer *(bira)* in Rhodes means lager, and the national brand, Fix, is normally cheaper than the German and Dutch imports. Most tourist bars and tavernas are more likely to offer Amstel, Henninger, Heineken and Carlsberg. Soft drinks *(anapsiktika)* such as Coca Cola and Seven Up are widely available, but can be very expensive, especially in the heart of resorts such as Líndhos. It is often better to stick to mineral water. The Greek soft drinks tend to be very sweet and syrupy; *Portokalada* is a fizzy orange drink, and the cloudy-looking *lemonada* has a real taste of lemon. Few bars serve freshly squeezed orange juice, but you can buy pure orange juice at mini-markets. Instant coffee – referred to

Feeling peckish? Doner kebab and pitta bread could fill the gap

simply as *nes* (short for Nescafé) – is widely available if the strong, thick Greek coffee is not to your liking, but specify when ordering. Coffee is taken on its own by most Greeks particularly after a meal, and is normally accompanied by a glass of water. Greek coffee comes very sweet *(glyko)* unless you ask for it to be medium *(metrio)* or without sugar *(sketo)*. You may find espresso in some of the more expensive cafés, while Scandinavian versions of coffee can be found in the new section of Rhodes Town. Tea is not widely drunk, but is available in tourist areas, though seldom accompanied by milk.

A popular pre-dinner drink is *ouzo*, the national aperitif – a clear, aniseed-flavoured spirit similar to Turkish *raki*. It is most commonly served mixed with cold water, when it turns a milky colour, but you can also have it neat or with ice.

SHOPPING

The Dodecanese islands were granted a special duty-free status, which they still enjoy, on their union with Greece in 1947. Even taking into account the cost of transport for imported goods, this means that shopping on Rhodes is excellent value – indeed, it is possible to buy quality goods at prices lower than in their country of origin. Popular souvenirs include leather bags and purses, brass and copper ware, worry beads of all sizes and materials, costume dolls, woven bedspreads, rugs and bags, shirts and dresses. Prices are fixed in the major shops and fashionable boutiques, but a little haggling – especially if you are buying several items in one shop – is considered the norm in the smaller shops.

SHOPPING

Rhodians are proud of their plates

Clothes

Cashmere, Harris tweed, worsteds, camel hair, flannel and, indeed, most top-quality British and European fabrics, are widely available. In Rhodes Town there are nearly 300 tailors who will make up garments for you in about three days. Shops specialising in sportswear include **Sportivo**, 22 Odhos G Griva, and **Rhodos Sport**, 15 Ethelondon Dodecanision; and in tee-shirts **Illusion T Shirts**, Odhos 25 Martiou.

Flowers

An excellent reasonably-priced flower shop, operated by the Municipality of Rhodes, can be found at Mandraki Harbour. It is open daily 07.00 to 14.30hrs.

Handicrafts

Embroidery and articles carved out of wood or onyx make popular souvenirs and are available throughout the island.

Jewellery

Goldsmiths and silversmiths have been practising their craft on Rhodes for 4,000 years, and there is an excellent choice available today, ranging from copies of jewellery made by ancient craftsmen to modern designs. The elaborate silver filigree jewellery of Rhodes, set with semi-precious stones imported from Italy, and made into rings, brooches, necklaces and other jewellery, is particularly distinctive and attractive. There are numerous jewellery shops throughout the island, especially in Rhodes Town. **M Mentos**, at 34 Odhos Apellou, in the Old Town, and **J Frantzis**, with branches at 103 Odhos Sokrátous and 19 Odhos Aristotelous, also in the Old Town, have good selections.

Lace

Handmade lace is a good bargain, especially that from Líndhos.

Leather

Handmade leather peasant boots from the village of Arkhángelos can be bought either there, or in Rhodes Town. They are very popular, not least because they are so comfortable. A good selection of leather handbags, belts and wallets can be found at **Telhines**, which has two shops in Rhodes Town – at 36/38 Odhos G Griva, and 10 Odhos Orfeos.

Pottery

Pottery from Líndhos is particularly attractive, especially the brightly coloured, decorative plates. But there are ceramic factories throughout the island which supply items to shops in all the main resorts, so there is a good choice everywhere. Most popular souvenirs, apart from plates, are vases and ashtrays. Blue tends to be the predominant colour, and designs are often based on deer, ships or flowers.

Photographic equipment

Brouzakis, 47 Odhos Sof Venizelou, Rhodes Town, has a good selection of photographic equipment including lenses, adaptors, and various types of filters. A quick film development service is also available.

Shoes

Fashionable shoes are made on the island. Those made for export, are of a higher quality, and make an excellent buy. Also good are leather slippers which have a reputation for being extremely hard wearing and long lasting. **Moshoutis**, in Iroon Polytechniou, has a good choice, as do the various branches of the chain '**24**', found in Ammokhostou, Karpathou and Makariou streets.

Spirits

All the better-known international brands of whisky, brandy, gin and other spirits and liqueurs can be bought very cheaply. **Cava Arapoudis**, 13 Odhos Gallias, Rhodes Town, is one of many outlets offering a good selection.

Lace-seller, Líndhos

Umbrellas

Colourful imported umbrellas and parasols are for sale practically everywhere. There is a good selection on offer at the **Umbrella Factory**, 41 Odhos Karpathou, Rhodes Town.

Wood

Olive-wood salad bowls, carving boards, mortars and pestles are worth seeking out in the better gift/souvenir shops.

Those who enjoy the hustle and bustle of markets should note that there are two in Rhodes Town – the Old Market (Palia Agorá), within the medieval walled city; and the larger New Market (Neá Agorá) at Mandraki Harbour.

ACCOMMODATION

Hotels

Hotels in Rhodes are classified according to the size of their rooms and public areas, the décor and furnishings of the rooms, and the facilities and service provided. 'Deluxe', 'A' and 'B' grade hotels have dining facilities on the premises; grade 'C' do not. Moves are currently under way by the Greek government to introduce a star system for hotels on the mainland and the islands in a bid to raise standards. Fears are also being expressed by many travel industry experts of the threat of too many hotels on Rhodes and other major Greek holiday islands. Plans have been submitted for no fewer than 264 new establishments in the Dodecanese within the next few years.

Hotel reservations can be made through a travel agent or airline, by writing to the hotel direct, or by contacting the Hotel Owners' Association of Rhodes, 8 Odhos Vas Sofias, Rhodes Town (tel: 26446).

If you arrive in Rhodes without accommodation, your best bet is to ask at the Tourist Office.

Pensions

First-class pensions are listed by the National Tourist Organisation. Bedrooms are functional and usually without private facilities, and represent the most reasonably priced hotel-style accommodation.

Rooms

A popular choice with independent travellers is to rent a room in a private house.

Líndhos, looking towards the sea

Rooms are generally clean, though with basic bathroom facilities. The option of a breakfast is sometimes made for a small additional charge. Beds may not be of the type most visitors are accustomed to. This is especially true in the resort of Líndhos where, in common with local traditions and habits, they are usually of the wooden platform type on which one or two mattresses are placed. A good night's sleep is not guaranteed!

The government-approved and categorised rooms are slightly more expensive than rooms in other households, but are of a reliable standard. This type of accommodation is seasonal, available mostly from May to September.

Self Catering

Eating out on Rhodes is cheap and good value so the freedom of a self catering holiday can be fully appreciated. The GNTO's guide to tour operators lists companies offering self catering.

The standards of accommodation on the island in self-catering properties are not comparable with those in other Mediterranean countries. Most tour operators try to ensure acceptable standards are maintained and that the accommodation offered is clean and comfortable, but luxuries such as electric kettles, toasters, irons and a vast choice of kitchen utensils will almost certainly not be included in the equipment provided in self-catering apartments and studios. Many apartments rely on solar heating systems; some have an electrical back-up system which is used only in bad weather. It is often necessary to contact the caretaker or owner if the weather is such that the electrical system needs to be used.

It has become standard practice for proprietors to ask to keep your passport, ostensibly for the police but in reality to prevent you leaving with an unpaid bill. Some owners may be satisfied with just taking down the details and they will almost always return the documents if you need them.

Water is a valuable commodity in Rhodes, especially in the height of the summer, and visitors should expect an occasional drop in water pressure. An increasing number of proprietors rely on solar power to heat the water. In such cases, when the sun is not shining, shortages of hot water have to be accepted.

Camping

Rhodes, with its wonderful climate, is ideal for camping. **St George's Camping** (or St George Tourist) at Lárdhos offers a superb range of facilities. Most of the tents provided are spacious and fully equipped. Located on a small road between Lárdhos and Líndhos, with terraced hills behind and sea views to the front, this is a lovely site. There is a huge swimming-pool with sun terraces, and an attractive restaurant and bar. There is also a supermarket for daily provisions. Sports enthusiasts can play table tennis or tennis, waterpolo, volleyball, pool games or occasional football matches. Evenings are catered for with barbecue nights, discos in the bar and occasional live entertainment. There is even a television lounge. Children have their own play area with swings and slides. When you want a change of scenery, the village of Pévka is about one and a half miles (2.5km) away, and Lárdhos itself about one mile (2km). The nearest beach, about 400 yards (360m) away, is pebbly. On site there are shower and wc blocks and a coin-operated launderette. Electricity is supplied to tent sites.

Faliraki Camping, just outside the resort of Falirakion, was opened in 1987 and, although less sophisticated than St George's, is also cheaper.

ENTERTAINMENT AND NIGHTLIFE

Most of the principal resorts on Rhodes have discothèques aimed mainly at younger visitors; this is especially so in Rhodes Town, Líndhos, Falirakion and Ixós. The majority of resorts also have a range of bars, from simple to stylish, with cocktail bars especially numerous. Folklore shows are staged frequently throughout the island, and versions of Zorba the Greek or Sirtaki dances can be seen in numerous tavernas, where the waiters will be happy to teach you a few basic steps. But you will soon want to sit down and admire when the professional dancers take to the floor and give more elaborate

performances, often including dancing in a ring of fire and lifting tables with their teeth.

Plate Smashing

As a sign of appreciation, happiness and high spirits, the Greeks may start to smash their plates on the floor. Officially, plate smashing has been declared illegal as it was considered likely to encourage rioting, but it can be seen at nightclubs and restaurants with special licences that allow the smashing of unglazed pottery. Plate smashing can be a wonderful way of letting off steam – but do not get carried away, since you are charged for each and every plate you break!

Cinemas

There are six cinemas in Rhodes Town, including the **Rodon**, to the rear of the National Theatre; the **Esperia**, in Odhos 25 Martiou; the **Metropol**, on Vironos, Vass Friderikis, Dimokratias and the junction with Stefanou Casouli; and the **Titania** on Odhos Kolokotroni east of the stadium. They show a mix of Greek and foreign films, accompanied by Greek subtitles.

Summer performances: 18.00–20.00, 20.00–22.00, and 22.00–24.00hrs; winter performances: 17.30–19.30, 19.30–21.30 and 21.30–23.30hrs. On Sundays and holidays performances usually start at 15.00hrs.

Discos

There are numerous discos centred on and around Platia Akadimas, in Rhodes Town, as well as Iroon Polytechniou, which branches north of Platia Akadimas and nearby Odhos Alexandrou Diakou. The other major resorts on the island also have discothèques.

Casino

If you like a flutter, there is one casino on Rhodes – at the Grand Hotel Astir Palace, in Rhodes Town. Here you can try your luck at American roulette, blackjack, *chemin-de-fer* and baccarat. There are also numerous slot machines. A passport is necessary to gain admittance, and dress must be smart – men must wear a shirt with collar.

Folk Shows

The **Greek Dance Group**, directed by Nelly Dimoglou, gives daily performances (except on Saturdays) of folk dances and songs in the **Old Theatre**, Odhos Andronicou, Rhodes Town, from May to October. Times of performances should be checked with the GNTO office or the Municipal Tourist Office.

The **National Theatre**, located at Mandraki Harbour, in the New Town, hosts plays and ballets based on folk customs, such as a wedding or the departure of sponge fishermen. Visiting companies from the National Theatre in Athens and the Athenian Festival also give performances here during the summer months.

Dancing the night away

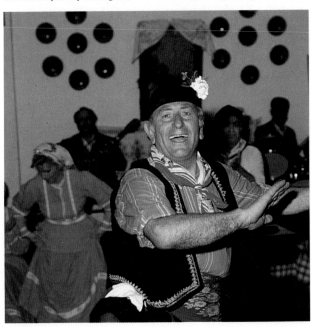

WEATHER AND WHEN TO GO

The climate of Rhodes is excellent most of the year, although the island is generally regarded as a summer holiday destination only, with the result that most hotels, restaurants, tavernas and bars close during the winter months.
Nevertheless, severe weather is a rarity, even in the coldest months – January and February (averaging 12°C/54°F). The most popular time for a holiday here is between July and August, but you can usually be sure of near-constant sunshine any time from May to October. In high summer, however, the climate is never unbearably hot, thanks to the *meltemi*, a northwest wind which provides a cool breeze, particularly on the west coast. An out-of-season visit – in April/May when the spring flowers are still blooming or September/October after the rush of visitors has left – has a great deal to recommend it.

What to Take and Wear

Good sunglasses are vital, as is suntan cream providing a good barrier to harmful ultra-violet rays. Clothing should be light, comfortable and casual, although more formal wear may be required at some of the more up-market hotels, especially in the evenings, and also if you plan to visit the casino in Rhodes Town. Bathing shoes are useful to avoid cuts from some of the rocky, pebbly beaches, and comfortable footwear advisable for those who intend to visit any of the ancient sites or undertake long walks. Sweaters are also advisable for most of the year, since the nights can be cool.

HOW TO BE A LOCAL

Like the majority of Greeks, Rhodians are friendly people who seldom seem to get ruffled or agitated and who, despite the pressures of tourism in the summer months, have a tendency to sit back and take things easy whenever the opportunity arises. They will linger for hours over a cup of strong, Greek coffee accompanied by a glass of water, chatting with friends and watching the world go by. A good place to join them is in Rhodes Town at one of the arcaded cafés overlooking Mandraki Harbour, or at one of the pastry/coffee shops in the New Town, or any of the unpretentious pavement cafés in the less developed resorts.
Like most Continentals, the Rhodians love food and eat out regularly – though they avoid

the 'touristy' restaurants in favour of simpler, less sophisticated tavernas. These are usually found in side streets or alleys – and this is where to search if you are looking for genuine local cuisine that is reasonably priced. They also love fish, which they buy from the fish stalls in the Neá Agorá (New Market) in Rhodes Town, directly from the quayside at several of the island's fishing villages, such as Kamiros Skala, or from vans which visit most of the bigger villages every weekday morning. Visitors who share their enjoyment of fish, and are staying in self-catering accommodation, would be well advised to follow suit.

For getting out and about, the locals rely heavily on buses which, though somewhat erratic, are frequent and cheap, so if you want to do some exploring, it makes sense to follow their example. Buses also let you see the traditional, non-touristy side of Rhodes, as they potter through remote villages. Scooters and motorcycles are also popular means of transport, especially with the younger generation, and are readily available for rent. Although helmets should be worn by law, few do so and they are seldom provided, so if you value your life this is the one case where it is not wise to follow local habits. Nudism is against Greek law, even though topless sunbathing is tolerated in most 'tourist' resorts on the island. However, should you decide to strip, your action could result in a fine or even lead to a prison sentence. The Rhodians are a modest

Locals travel at their own pace

people, and visitors should have regard for local custom. It is considered bad form for men or women to wear shorts in churches or museums. Women should wear a scarf in church.

CHILDREN

Rhodes is popular with people with children and is well equipped to cater for them. Many hotels have separate children's swimming-pools, or areas of the main pool reserved for their use, and some of the larger establishments have children's play areas and offer children's menus and special programmes of games and activities. High chairs and early

CHILDREN

dinners are also widely
available. A large number of
hotels on the islands have
three-sided lifts (ie with no
inner door), a danger to
unsupervised children. These
have been mentioned in hotel
descriptions throughout the
book. Many of the island's
beaches offer safe bathing, and
are well equipped with
watersports facilities.
Parents should take note,
however, that the cooling
west-coast wind can mask high
temperatures, so that they may
underrate the power of the sun.
Children should be protected
from sunburn at all times and
should wear a hat.
At night, most children are
generally fascinated with the
Greek evenings laid on at
numerous tavernas and hotels
throughout the island – and

*Restaurants and cafés do their best
to accommodate children*

especially enjoy the opportunity
for intentional plate smashing!
(See page 100.)
For children who prefer
burgers and fries to Greek food,
Rhodes surpasses many of its
competitors, since many
establishments feature precisely
this type of food on their menus.
Most children also love pizza
and spaghetti, and again these
are widely available. The
Greeks love children, so there
is no problem in taking them out
to eat with you.
It should not be necessary to
bring baby requisites with you,
as the shops on Rhodes can
supply the usual items, such as
disposable napkins or milk
powder.
Many hotels provide baby

listening or babysitting services. Such facilities have been mentioned in the descriptions of individual hotels in the book. If this is important to the success of your stay, check that the service is available before booking.

TIGHT BUDGET

As is the case with many holiday destinations, Rhodes is cheapest in the low seasons. Most of the hotels, restaurants and bars on the island are closed during the winter months – though, surprisingly, the museums and the ancient sites remain open – so the best time to enjoy a holiday on Rhodes, and save on expense, is in the spring and autumn, when hotel and holiday package rates are often less expensive than during the peak summer months of July and August.

Where to Stay

You can also cut the cost of a holiday in Rhodes by opting for self-catering accommodation. The island offers a wide range of apartments and studios for holiday rental, especially in the smaller, less-developed resorts, and most of them are available through overseas tour operators. These are invariably cheaper than hotels, especially if several adults are sharing.

An inexpensive option for the lone traveller, or couple, is to stay in a pension or rent a room in a private house. Another tip is to avoid the well-developed resorts and choose instead one of the lesser-known, off-the-beaten-track places. Not only will you find these offer less

expensive accommodation, but prices in restaurants and bars are usually lower than in the more popular, livelier resorts.

Where to Eat

To save on restaurant bills, seek out the less-expensive self-service restaurants and cafeterias, especially in Rhodes Town. The market here is a fruitful source of cheap tavernas. In general, the best value taverna is where you see locals eating. A picnic lunch of bread, cheese and fruit is cheap – and healthy. Or you can go for some of the delicious take-away snacks, available from bakers – *tiropites* (cheese pies) are delicious and ubiquitous.

Getting About

Buses are a cheap mode of transport and cover the whole island. However, in season they tend to be very crowded, and out of season services are much less regular than in the height of summer. Taxis are not such an expensive alternative as in many other places – especially when shared by a few. Fix a price with the driver before setting off on an excursion. Scooter or moped rental is not too costly and a practical way of getting to see everything. See **Directory – Driving** for more information.

In Brief

- Travel out of high season.
- Avoid popular resorts.
- Stay in pensions, private rooms or self-catering accommodation.
- Eat where the locals go.
- Use public transport.

SPECIAL EVENTS

1 January. On New Year's Day – or St Basil's Day as it is also known – visitors might be offered sprigs of the herb basil, named after the saint, as a symbol of hospitality.

6 January. Epiphany Day, marked by the blessing of water throughout Greece. In Rhodes Town a cross blessed by a bishop is dropped into the harbour and young swimmers try to retrieve it, while white pigeons are released to fly over the area. The person to surface with the cross is anointed with oil, blessed, and given coins.

February. Carnival time, with floats, fancy dress and merrymaking in Rhodes Town, Arkhángelos, Apóllona and the fishing village of Kamiros Skala.

Easter. This is the most important festival of the Greek Orthodox Church. For the three weeks preceding Lent, there are colourful processions and raucous parties, with the revellers donning costumes and masks. The first Monday of Lent, known as Clean Monday, is a day of fasting when some people eat only garlic mashed with potatoes. On Good Friday a solemn, silent procession takes place in Rhodes Town, while Holy Saturday marks the beginning of Easter. Church bells peal, fireworks are set off, and worshippers exchange Easter greetings.

25 March. Greek Independence Day. This is a national holiday with parades and folk dancing.

1 May. May Day, when garlands of flowers are hung on doorknobs often by lovers. They usually remain in place for many weeks.

15 May. A giant street market, fiesta and funfair is held on this day to mark the Festival of the Virgin Mary.

24 June. The feast of St John the Baptist, celebrated everywhere with bonfires.

June. The last 10 days mark the island's annual summer celebrations, with beauty contests, folk dancing and singing.

July. The first week is Naval Week, with open-air concerts and fireworks as well as boat races.

30 July. In honour of St Saul, a big celebration is held near the village of Soroní. Saul is said to have been a companion of St Paul and to have performed miracles. The celebrations are lively, and include donkey racing and folk dancing.

6 August and throughout the month. Dance festivals take place in the villages of Maritsá, Kalithiaí and Embonas.

15 August. Assumption Day, the most renowned festival in the Dodecanese, with week-long dancing and religious processions in Kremastí and Triánda.

8 September. Birth of the Virgin Mary. At Tsambika, on the eve of this holy day, childless women make a pilgrimage up the steep hill to the monastery to pray for fertility.

28 October. Parades, folk dances and other celebrations are held throughout the island to mark the Greek victory over Fascist Italy in 1940.

SPORT

Rhodes offers a good choice of sporting and recreational activities, ranging from excellent watersports to hiking and golf.

Boating

If you are a competent sailor and wish to take a boat out for a day or longer, you can apply to the Nautical Club of Rhodes (NOR), at 9 Platia Kountourioutou (near the Elli Beach Club), tel: 23287. It is important to remember, however, that the unpredictable north wind known as the *meltemi* can make sailing in small boats quite tricky.

Fishing

Spear-fishing is very popular on the island, and you do not need a permit. However, you are not allowed to practise the sport within 100 yards (90m) of a public beach, and any fish you spear must weigh more than 150 grams. You can snorkel freely anywhere along the coast, but for sub-aqua sports you need to join the diving school in Rhodes harbour. The best fishing grounds tend to be off the shores of Líndhos, Kamiros, Kallithéa and Yennádhion, and fishing tackle can be bought in the Neá Agorá, Rhodes Town.

Sitting on the dock of a bay

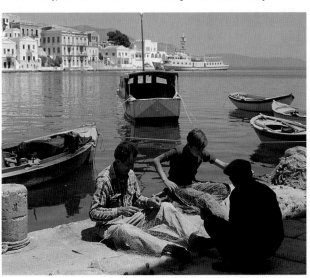

SPORT

Golf

There is only one golf course on Rhodes, an 18-hole course situated at Afándou village, just over 12 miles (20km) from Rhodes Town (tel: 51255). Facilities include a clubhouse, changing rooms, and a snack bar. Clubs can be hired, and green fees are not expensive by international standards. Many hotels on the east and west coasts have mini-golf courses, which can also be found in Rhodes Town (near the Palm Hotel) and on the west coast (near the Metropolitan Capsis Hotel) where visitors not staying in hotels can play.

Horse Riding

Mikes Stables, inland from Kalithiaí village, about nine miles (15km) from Rhodes Town.

Hunting

A licence is required to hunt game or animals, such as wild duck, hares and partridges. Applications should be made to the **Hunting Club of Rhodes**, Municipal Marketplace, 1st Floor, No 7 (tel: 21841). The hunting season runs from 25 August to 10 March for migratory birds, and from 1 November to 10 January for rabbits and partridges. Although the deer population is quite large, they are protected by law, and cannot be hunted.

Tennis

Numerous hotels on the island have their own tennis courts. Visitors staying in smaller, less well equipped hotels, can play at the **Rhodes Town Tennis Club** (tel: 25705), located at 20 Vassileos Konstantinou, facing Elli Beach. This welcomes all non-nationals who wish to play. There are seven courts in total, of which two are clay and the remainder cement. The courts are open between 09.00 and 20.00hrs. Players must wear tennis clothes – swimsuits are not allowed. Racquets and balls are available for hire.

Walking

In the spring and autumn Rhodes is an ideal island for walking, providing routes for both serious ramblers and those who like a gentle stroll. There is a dearth of official information but an invaluable source of information is Noel Rochford's *Landscapes of Rhodes* (Sunflower Books).

Water Sports

Most of the island's popular beaches offer facilities for windsurfing, waterskiing and para-skiing. There is an excellent windsurfing school – the **Surfers Paradise** – opposite the Hilton Hotel, Ixós, and others at Falirakion Beach and near the Lindos Bay Hotel. Pedaloes can be hired at most beaches. The east coast is more suited to waterskiing than the west, the sea and wind here being calmer. Swimming is understandably the most popular of all watersports, and is best practised at resorts such as Falirakion, whose beach slopes gently out to sea, making it an ideal swimming spot for children; Líndhos, where there are excellent changing facilities and showers; or Lárdhos Bay, where the long, sandy beach is less crowded.

DIRECTORY

Contents

Arriving

By Air

Although a few scheduled airlines operate direct, non-stop flights from European cities to Rhodes, the majority of flights are routed via Athens, with onward connections to Rhodes. At Athens, Olympic Airways – which has the monopoly of internal Greek flights – operates from the West Air Terminal of the Hellenikon Airport. If you arrive on a foreign airline, take one of the frequent buses from the East Air Terminal. The flight from Athens to Rhodes takes about one and a half hours. In addition to the scheduled flights, numerous companies operate package holidays to Rhodes incorporating a direct charter flight and accommodation in either hotels or self-catering apartments, studios, or village rooms. All flights to Rhodes land at Rhodes International Airport, which is located at Paradhísion, about 10 miles (16km) from Rhodes Town. It has all the usual facilities of a busy airport including a tourist office.

From the airport you can reach Rhodes Town either by bus or taxi. The latter are easy to obtain and are reasonably priced, but it is wise to confirm the price in advance.

Olympic Airways' buses have the edge over the public variety because they have greater luggage capacity. Public buses run every 45 minutes from 06.30 to 22.30hrs. Porters are available to carry bags to the taxi rank or bus stop. If you wish to use the Olympic Airways bus to take you to the airport on your journey home, you must wait in front of the airline's office at 19 Odhos Ierou Lohou (tel: 24571) at least two hours before the flight departure time.

By Sea

There are sea routes to Athens from Genoa, Venice, Ancona, Naples, Brindisi, Bari and Marseilles. Vessels operating on these routes are generally large passenger ships, many equipped to carry cars. Rhodes

DIRECTORY

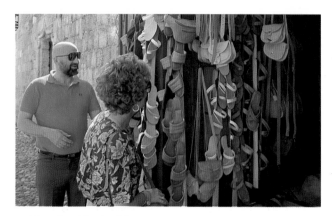

Leather goods are popular souvenirs

and the other islands of the Dodecanese are served by scheduled passenger and car ferry boats from Piraeus, near Athens. Frequency varies according to the season. In the peak summer months one or more vessels a day leave for Rhodes. Some of these carry cargo as well as passengers , so be prepared for delays when loading or unloading takes longer than expected. The services tend to be extremely busy, and cabins should be booked well in advance, even in the low season.

By Road

There is a variety of land–sea routes to Rhodes across Europe though they are not the quickest or most comfortable means of reaching the island. The usual route from Britain is from one of the Channel ports to either Ostend or Zeebrugge, continuing to Athens by way of Brussels, Cologne, Munich, Salzburg, Belgrade and Nis. The journey by bus takes three and a half days.

By Rail

You can travel to Rhodes by a combination of rail and ship, but it is a long journey and not really recommended. The most popular route is via Brussels, Munich, Belgrade and Athens.

Entry Formalities

A passport but no visa is required for visitors to Rhodes from West European countries (including UK citizens), Australia, New Zealand, Canada, the US and Irish Republic.

Visas are also generally not required by:

military persons travelling on a Military Identity Card (with movement or leave order) issued by NATO; holders of a re-entry permit provided that they hold official documents proving their residence in Greece; holders of tickets with onward reservations provided that their journey to a third country will commence within 48 hours from arrival. It should be noted, however, that if you leave the airport you need a visa. Check regulations before your journey.

If you want to stay longer than three months you should officially apply for an extension. In Rhodes this can be done through the local police. It is advisable to complete this procedure a couple of weeks before your time runs out and also to keep all your pink, personalised bank exchange slips as confirmation that you can subsist without working. If you plan to visit Turkey from Rhodes there are one or two important rules to follow to avoid re-entry or exit problems. Check with a local travel agent or tour operator's representative.

Camping

The island offers two camp sites, both of which have excellent amenities including shops, sports and entertainment facilities. They are St George's Camping (tel: 44249), located at Lárdhos Village, about 5½ miles (9km) from Lárdhos, on the east coast; and Faliraki Camping, (tel: 85516), situated just outside the village of Falirakion, also on the east coast. For more details see **Accommodation** page 99. Note that it is illegal to camp outside official campsites.

Chemists see **Pharmacies**

Crime

Crime is rare on Rhodes, but it is still wise to take precautions such as depositing valuables in the hotel safe, if available, and taking care of your possessions when in public, especially on the beach or when shopping. In the event of theft contact the police at Etgelondon Dodekanissiou, Rhodes Town (tel: 27423), or your nearest police station.

Drug offences can lead to heavy sentences. Other activities that can get the unwary traveller into trouble are taking photographs in sensitive areas such as military barracks (usually marked with a camera crossed through) and abusing the Greek flag.

See also **Driving – Regulations** for certain legal requirements to be observed by motorists.

Customs

Visitors aged 18 years and over are allowed to import free of duty the following items:

If arriving from EC countries: 300 cigarettes **or** 75 cigars or 150 cigarillos **or** 400 grams of tobacco; one and a half litres of alcohol **or** five litres of wine, sparkling wine or liqueurs; 75 grams of perfume and three-eighths of a litre of toilet water; 1,000 grams of coffee **or** 375 grams of coffee extract; 200 grams of tea **or** 75 grams of tea extract.

If arriving from non EC countries: 200 cigarettes **or** 50 cigars **or** 100 cigarillos **or** 250 grams of tobacco; one litre of alcohol **or** two litres of wines, sparkling wines or liqueurs; 50 grams of perfume and a quarter of a litre of toilet water; 500 grams of coffee **or** 200 grams of coffee extract; 100 grams of tea **or** 40 grams of tea extract.

Visitors to Greece may, as a general rule, temporarily import personal articles duty-free, providing they are considered

DIRECTORY

as being in use and in keeping with the personal status of the importer. Plants with soil are prohibited. Cats and dogs require health and rabies inoculation certificates issued by a veterinary authority in the country of origin not more than 12 months (cats six months) and not less than six days prior to arrival. Importation of antiquities and works of art is free but they should be declared, together with their value, so that they may be freely exported. It is forbidden to export antiquities and works of art found in Greece. The duty-free allowance for goods exported from Greece will depend upon the traveller's nationality and the import regulations of the country of their destination, which should be determined before departure.

Disabled People

Little specific provision is made, but some accommodation is built with access needs in mind. The Greek National Tourist Organisation should have details of specialist travel companies if local travel agencies are unable to help. Once in Rhodes you should find the locals welcoming and helpful.

Driving

Main roads are usually asphalted, but it is folly to drive at speed. Curves are not usually signposted and seldom banked, so great care is required. Secondary roads are sometimes very rough, and are often narrow, serpentine and steep.

Fuel

Filling stations are open from 07.00 to 19.00hrs Monday to Saturday, and they operate a rota system to cover evenings until midnight and Sundays. There is always a station open somewhere near Rhodes Town, but out of town supplies are patchy. Petrol (leaded) is sold as Venzini Apli (91-92 octane) and Venzini Super (96-98 octane). Unleaded petrol is sold as Super (95 octane) at stations displaying the sign. The acceptance of credit cards for petrol purchases is limited.

Regulations

Vehicles are driven on the right-hand side of the road and, unless otherwise indicated by signs, cars are subject to the following speed restrictions: 50kph (31mph) in built-up areas; 80kph (49mph) outside built-up areas; and 100kph (62mph) on dual-carriageways. Seat belts must be worn by law – though many rented cars are not even fitted with them. It is also compulsory to carry a warning triangle, fire extinguisher and a first-aid kit – failure to comply may result in a fine. Children are not allowed to travel in the front seat of a car, and it is an offence to carry a petrol can in a car.

Rental

Bicycles, mopeds, motorcycles and cars are popular means of exploring the island and are readily available in Rhodes Town, Falirakion, Triánda, Líndhos and several smaller resorts. There is no shortage of rental firms, including well known companies such as Avis and Hertz in Rhodes Town, and local firms in all the major resorts. No licence is required for mopeds or motorcycles up to 125cc. It is important to remember that the basic insurance offered on the hire of mopeds or motorcycles provides only third party insurance cover – meaning that neither rider nor the bike is covered – so drivers should take out a comprehensive policy, especially in view of the poor state of many of the roads. Most companies have clauses in their conditions of hire which stipulate that their insurance is invalidated if you travel on non-tarmac roads (many sites can be reached only on rough tracks). It should also be noted that motorcycles are not allowed in towns after 23.00hrs. For driving on Rhodes a valid pink EC licence, which includes translations, is acceptable. An International Driving Permit (IDP) is advisable for holders of other licences, such as the British green licence, because these do not carry translations. An IDP is also required for nationals of the US, Canada and Australia. The IDP is best

The freedom of the road can be enjoyed on two wheels

DIRECTORY

Bright lights and quiet streets

obtained from a motoring club at home. A registration document and a green card insurance are also required for temporarily imported vehicles. To drive your own imported car or motorcycle over 50cc, the minimum age is 17, but you have to be 23 years old to rent a vehicle, though many companies do not stick rigidly to this rule.

Electricity

The voltage in Rhodes, as in the rest of Greece, is 220 volts. Transformers are not usually required, but as plugs are of the common European two-pin type, an adapter may be necessary in order to use a shaver or hairdrier. Street lights are scarce in some parts of the island, so it is useful to take a torch with you, especially if you are staying in an apartment or pension off the beaten track.

Embassies and Consulates

There are a number of West European consulates on Rhodes, but the US, Australia, New Zealand, Canada and the Republic of Ireland do not have consulates here.

Australia: 37 Dimitriou Soutsou Street, Ambelokipi, Athens (tel: 644-7307)

Canada: 4 Ioannou, Gennadiou Street, Athens (tel: 723-9511)

New Zealand: 15-17 An Tsoha Street, Ambelokipi, Athens (tel: 641-0311)

Republic of Ireland: 7 Leoforos Vasileos, Konstantinou, Athens (tel: 723-2771)

UK: 23 Odhos 25 Martiou, Rhodes Town (tel: 27306/27247)

US: Vas Sofia 91, Athens (tel: 721-2951)

Emergency Telephone Numbers

Police: 100
Fire: 199
Ambulance: 166
Hospital emergency: 25555
Greek Automobile Association: 24377

Entertainment Information

The English-language *Rhodes Gazette*, published from April to the end of October, contains information on local events and entertainment, and is available free from newsagents and tourist offices.

Entry Formalities see Arriving

Health

There are no required inoculations for Rhodes, or other parts of Greece, but it is a sensible precaution to have a typhoid-cholera booster and to ensure you are up to date on tetanus and polio. British (upon production of Department of health form E111) and other EC nationals are entitled to free medical care, but this means admittance only to the lowest grade of hospital, and does not include nursing care. In any case, treatment and prescribed medicines are first paid for and the costs are then refunded by the Greek authorities. If you require prolonged medical care or are from a country outside the EC you will need to make use of private treatment, which is expensive, so travel insurance to cover this is an essential precaution.

Medical Services

The Greek Red Cross has recently set up a round-the-clock medical advice service for hotels throughout the mainland and the islands. The service links hotels with a Red Cross centre in Athens, where a team of 10 doctors, selected for their knowledge of languages, works on a shift system providing free advice on medical emergencies. Where required, it will indicate the most suitable hospital for treatment of a specific emergency. The aim is to cut down on delays in providing treatment, either locally or in the nearest suitable hospital.

Most doctors pride themselves on their English. Look for the sign IATPEION, indicating a doctor's clinic or surgery. Dentist: Antony Alaxouzos, 40 Odhos Amerikis, Rhodes Town (tel: 28459).

Minor Illnesses

You can buy across-the-counter medicines at pharmacies in the major resorts to treat any minor accident or illness, but it is worth taking a small medical kit including an analgesic, first aid dressings and something to soothe insect bites. Minor stomach upsets should be treated with water and re-hydration salts.

Mosquitoes

The very hot climate of Rhodes is, as one would expect, the kind that attracts reptiles, insects – mosquitoes included – and a variety of other animal life. These are not dangerous, although mosquitoes are often a real nuisance. It is advisable to take precautions to avoid this irritating creature from causing you any discomfort. The most effective way is by using tablets with electrical hotplates. You simply plug them in overnight in a ventilated area, away from draughts. Alternatively, coils which you leave to smoulder like incense sticks, as well as sprays, are also available; sprays are best applied just before dark, with the windows closed for a while. When out of doors you can use an insect repellent; some are in roll-on form, like deodorants.

Sunburn

Sunburn can also be a major health problem, so make sure you use a good barrier cream and go for a steady tan; remember, even when the breeze blows you can still burn.

Water

Although the water is considered quite safe to drink, most visitors prefer to avoid tap water and ice and use bottled water, which is available at all bars, restaurants, hotels and supermarkets.

Holidays

On public and religious holidays most shops close for the day; they also close the afternoon before and the morning after a religious holiday. If a national holiday falls on a Sunday it is the following Monday which is observed. Note that the Greek Orthodox Easter can fall several weeks before or after the Catholic Easter. The following are public holidays:
1 January; 6 January (Epiphany); 25 March (Independence Day); Orthodox Good Friday, Easter Sunday and Easter Monday (March/April); 1 May (Labour Day); Whit Monday (May/June);

15 August (Feast of the Assumption); 28 October (Okhi Day) – commemorating when, in 1940, Greece rejected Mussolini's ultimatum and entered the war on the side of the Allies; 24 December (St Stephen's Day); Christmas Day and Boxing Day.

Lost Property

For property lost in your hotel, report to the management or travel representative in the first instance, and then to the local police station. For articles lost elsewhere, contact the police on 100 or visit the police station in Rhodes Town.

Media

Newspapers

Overseas newspapers are available in Rhodes about a day after publication. They are obtainable in and around Mandraki Harbour, in Rhodes Town, and also in some of the larger hotels. For faster news in English, look out for *Athens News*, published daily except Mondays. The magazine *Where and What* gives general information in English, German and Swedish, while the English-language newspaper *Rhodes Gazette*, published from April to the end of October, is available at the tourist office. Most hotels sell newspapers and magazines, but for the biggest selection of foreign periodicals try the news-stand in the arcaded entrance to the market-place at Mandraki Harbour, or alternatively the bookstalls in front of the main post office.

Radio

Some Greek radio stations

sometimes have programmes of interest to the foreign listener. ERT1 located at 1008KHz and 297.6m or 91.80MHz, presents the news in English daily at 07.40hrs, preceded by a weather forecast and sea conditions programme at 06.30hrs. ERT2, on 981KHz and 305.8m, has two newscasts daily in English and French, going out at 14.20 and 21.20hrs. To receive the BBC World Service, tune to the 49 metres band on short wave; in the evening, try medium wave.

Television

There are nine television channels including two Greek, one Turkish, one German, one French, one English/American, and one continuous news. The channels ERT 1 and 2 show numerous programmes and films in English with Greek subtitles.

Money Matters

The unit of currency is the drachma. The most common notes in circulation are those of 50, 500, 1,000 and 5,000 drachmas, and coins of 1 and 2 drs (bronze), 5, 10 and 20 drs (nickel) and 50 drs (gold/bronze). The drachma is theoretically subdivided into 100 lepta, though devaluation has considerably reduced the value of one drachma, and in practice the lepta is never encountered. You are officially allowed to take just 100,000 drachmas into Rhodes with you. Upon your return, no more than 20,000 drachmas may be taken out of Greece. There are no restrictions on the import or export of foreign currency up to

National costume is worn with pride

the equivalent of $1,000 but amounts in excess of this must be declared to the Currency Control Authorities on your arrival in Rhodes.

Exchange

Most visitors take their money in the form of travellers' cheques, but a small amount of local currency is worth acquiring in advance, especially if arriving at weekends when banks and some currency exchange offices will be closed. Cash, travellers' cheques and Eurocheques can be exchanged at banks and post offices. The rate of exchange varies from day to day, but is the same at all banks and post offices. Eurocheques must be made out in drachmas, and you pay a commissioning charge of around 1.6 per cent to the exchanging bank, plus a handling fee per transaction. Travellers' cheques are also widely accepted in shops and restaurants, but at lower exchange rates than banks. Most major credit cards are fairly widely accepted in the larger resorts, but only by the more expensive shops, hotels and restaurants. They are particularly useful for large purchases, like renting cars, but are no use in tavernas.

Banks

The major Greek banks, including the National Bank of Greece, the Commercial Bank

Enjoying coffee and conversation

of Greece, the Bank of Greece and the Ionian and Popular, have branches in Rhodes Town. In the Old Town are: Commercial Bank, Platia Moussiou; Ionian and Popular Bank, Platia Símis; National Bank of Greece, Platia Moussiou. New Town: National Bank of Greece, Platia Kiprou; Bank of Greece, Mandraki Harbour. Cash may be obtained at the National Bank for Eurocard and Visa holders, and at the Commercial Bank for Diners Club holders. If you lose money, contact the police and take your passport with you. The police will give you a form to forward to your insurance company.

If you travel to Turkey from Rhodes, remember that you cannot obtain Turkish currency in Greece or exchange Greek currency for Turkish when you get there. You should either arm yourself with some American dollars – which can be obtained from Greek banks – or cash one of your own travellers' cheques on arrival.

Opening Times

Shops: those selling jewellery, cosmetics, records and cassettes, leather goods and shoes are usually open daily, including holidays, 08.00–13.00hrs and again 17.00–22.00hrs; Sundays 10.00–14.00hrs. Other shops, and dry-cleaners, open Monday to Friday 08.00–13.00hrs and again 17.00–21.00hrs; Saturdays 08.00–13.00hrs; Sundays and holidays 10.00–14.00hrs.

Banks: Monday to Friday 08.00–14.00hrs, and also Saturday mornings for the exchange of currency and/or travellers' cheques. In summer some banks open Monday to Friday 08.00–13.00hrs and 17.00–21.00hrs; Saturdays 08.00–13.00hrs.

Car Repair Workshops: Monday to Saturday 07.30–15.30hrs; closed Sundays and holidays

Hairdressers: Women's – Monday to Friday 09.00–21.00hrs; Saturdays 09.00–20.00hrs; Sundays and holidays 09.00–12.00hrs. Men's – Monday to Friday 08.00–21.00hrs; Saturdays 09.00–19.00hrs. Closed Sundays and holidays.

Museums and Sites: Most museums and places of interest open Tuesday to Saturday 08.30–15.00hrs; Sundays and holidays 08.30–15.00hrs. Closed Mondays. All are closed on 25 December, 1 January, 25 March, Good Friday and Easter.

Nightclubs: All close at 02.30hrs at the latest.

Restaurants: Lunch 11.00–15.00hrs; dinner 18.00hrs till midnight.

Personal Safety

Watch out for the lethal three-sided lifts fitted in many hotels in Rhodes. These lifts have no inner door, so as they move, passengers run the risk of abrasion or worse against the wall. A few lifts carry signs warning children not to use the lift without an adult present, but it is advisable to take extra care. Many hotel swimming-pools fail to have depth markings, so care is required here, too, especially

DIRECTORY

Greek Orthodox priest

with children.

Women travellers to Rhodes should not be troubled by sexual harassment from local males, as Greek men, particularly away from the main tourist spots, are generally respectful of women. A firm 'no' is usually enough to deter anyone making advances.

Pharmacies

Known as *Farmakia*, they can be identified by their sign of a red or blue cross on a white background. A rota system is in operation throughout the island, so there is always one pharmacy open at any time of day or night. You can obtain the address of the nearest duty pharmacy from your hotel desk or by contacting the Police. Most are open from 08.30 to 13.30/14.30hrs Monday to Saturday, and also from 17.00 to 20.00hrs on Sundays. The

majority of pharmacies provide the normal remedies and are happy to give advice on minor ailments. Most items are available without prescription, although medicines are not particularly cheap.

Places of Worship
Roman Catholic Churches: at St Mary's, off Odhos Kaphopoule, a mass is said in Latin on weekdays (and on Saturdays in the tourist season) at 19.00hrs and on Sundays at 08.00, 11.00 and 19.00hrs; and at St Francis's, 28 Odhos Dimokratias, services are held on Sundays at 10.00 and on weekdays at 08.30hrs. **Protestant services** are held occasionally at St Mary's, conducted by visiting clergymen.
Jewish: the 17th-century Sholom Synagogue, in Odhos Dosiadou, is open for prayer.

Police
The police (called *chorofilakes*) have green uniforms and deal with normal, civilian problems including those of tourists. Police headquarters are near the main post office on Platia Eleftherias, in Rhodes Town.

Post Office
The main post office on Rhodes can be found on Platia Eleftherias at Mandraki Harbour in Rhodes Town, and there is another, in the Old Town, on Odhos Orfeos.
Sending letters or postcards by surface mail can take a considerable time. Airmail is quicker, but even by this method letters take three to six days to reach the rest of Europe, five to eight days to

reach North America, and a little longer to Australia and New Zealand. Postcards can be very slow indeed: up to two weeks for Europe, a month to North America or the Pacific. A modest fee for express service cuts letter delivery time to about two days for the UK and three days for North America. There is a basic fee for airmail letters (the first 20 grams within Europe, the first 10 grams for North America), then a further fee for successive weight division (20–50 grams for Europe, 10–20 grams for North America).

Parcels must be taken to a post office for inspection and wrapped afterwards, so take wrapping paper, sticky-tape, string, scissors and a pen with you.

Opening times: main branch, 08.00–20.00hrs in summer, 08.00–19.00hrs in winter; Old Town Office, Monday to Friday 08.00–20.00hrs, Saturdays and Sundays 09.00–18.00hrs. Reception desks of the larger hotels normally sell postage stamps, and post boxes are yellow and black with a hunting horn design.

Public Transport

Buses

Rhodes Town is the centre of public transport, and buses from here go all over the island, which is well served by roads. Services are fairly regular and inexpensive, but buses tend to become very crowded in the high season, and are much less frequent out of season and on Sundays and holidays. Two companies – KTEL and RODA – provide the local bus services. KTEL operates along the east coast, while the west coast is RODA territory. The two lines meet only rarely. The two bus stations are within a hundred metres or so of each other at the back of the New Market. The KTEL concourse is beside the Municipal Gardens; RODA departures are from Odhos Averof, immediately behind the New Market. In addition, there

Playing backgammon in a kaferion

are five city buses which run until 22.00 or 23.00hrs. Buses to the airport depart approximately every 45 minutes from the Olympic Airways premises on the left of Odhos Ierou Lohou, beyond the Plaza Hotel. Tickets are bought on the bus before departure; it may be worth purchasing a day pass.

Boats

The main passenger ferry port on the island is the Commercial Harbour. There are scheduled stopping services to all of the Dodecanese islands as well as to Piraeus, Crete and Turkey. The journey time depends on the number of ports of call. There is a faster hydrofoil service, known as the Flying Dolphin, which operates services in the high season to Kos, Simi and Pátmos. From Mandraki Harbour some tour companies operate small coastal vessels for day trips to other destinations along the coast, including Líndhos. Caïque trips to Khálki leave from Kamiros Skala in season. Seats can be booked though the agent at 2 Odhos Papagou, opposite the KTEL bus station. The bigger boats are served by the DANE agency, 95 Odhos Amerikis (tel: 30930), and the Kydon Agency, Etgelondon Dodekanissiou (tel: 23000).

Taxis

Taxis are privately owned, but can be booked by telephoning 27666. This is the number of the main taxi rank in Rhodes Town, in Platia Rimini, at Mandraki Harbour. In rural areas, the type of taxi used is known as an *agoreon*. This has no meter,

rates being fixed for specific distances or zones.

Senior Citizens

Many travel companies offer attractive rates to senior citizens booking an out-of season holiday of several weeks – contact your travel agent for information. Outside the hustle and bustle of the main holiday season, when the weather is more temperate, the natural beauty of the island offers much for older visitors to enjoy. They would be well advised to avoid the bigger, longer-established resorts, however, where noise could be troublesome.

Student and Youth Travel

Students of any age should obtain an International Student Identity Card, ensuring discounts not only in respect of travel, but also on entry to museums, archaeological sites and some forms of entertainment on Rhodes. Anyone under 26 years of age, but not a student, may consider applying for membership of the Federation of International Youth Travel Organisation, which guarantees discounts from some ferry and tour operators.

Telephones

You can make a phone call from one of the two OTE (Organismos Telephikinonion Ellathos – Greek Telecommunications Organisation) offices in Rhodes Town, or from a call box. The central office of the OTE is located at the corner of Amerikis and 25 Martiou streets. There are ten direct-dial telephones available in service seven days a week, from 06.00hrs until midnight, from April to October; at other times the service closes at 23.00hrs. International calls are metered, and you pay the cashier after your call. Blue and red phones you see elsewhere are for local calls; orange ones for long distance. International direct dialling is prefixed by the code 00 followed by the country code (1 for the US and Canada, 44 for the UK, 61 for Australia, 64 for New Zealand and 353 for the Republic of Ireland), area code and number. An English-speaking operator can help on 162. To call Britain, for example, dial 00 44, the area code without the initial 0, and then the number. To call Rhodes from overseas, dial the international code for Greece (01030), followed by 241, for Rhodes, followed by the number you require.

An icon glistens in a roadside shrine

Useful Numbers

Rhodes Telephone Code: 0241
English-speaking International Operator: 162
Fire Brigade: 199
Greek National Tourism Organisation: 23255, 23655
Líndhos Telephone Code: 0244
Líndhos Information Office: 31428 Municipality Information Office: 35945
Olympic Airways' Office: 24571/5
Port Authority: 28888, 22220
Recorded instructions for international calls: 169
Telephone information: local, 131; international, 161
Weather: 149

Time

Greek time is two hours ahead of Greenwich Mean Time and British Summer Time, except for short periods in the spring and autumn when Greek clocks are changed in advance of British clocks. Local time is seven hours ahead of US and Canada Eastern Time, and eight hours behind Australian and New South Wales Time.

Tipping

By law, service charges are included in the bills at hotels, tavernas and restaurants. However, a little extra is expected if good service has been provided. In general, 10 per cent is a satisfactory amount to leave as a tip.

Toilets

Greek plumbing leaves a lot to

DIRECTORY

be desired. The ancient Greeks may have been the pioneers of civilisation, but the new generation are certainly low on the list in the plumbing league ... although, to be fair, things have considerably improved in recent years. However, with the influx of tourists, some anomalies in the plumbing systems are bound to occur throughout the season, especially during July and August. Small hotels and pension-type places usually request guests to place used toilet paper in a pedal bin. The reason is that the pipes are narrow, so if you fail to follow the instructions you block the lavatory. Rhodes Town has several public toilets, generally reasonably clean and well maintained. They can be found in the Neá Agorá (New Market), at Mandraki Harbour; on Odhos Alexandrou Papagou, near the bus terminus; at the offices of Olympic Airways, in Odhos Ierou Lohou, in the New Town; and, in the Old Town, in Odhos Orfeos between the Grand Masters' Palace Gates and the Clock Tower.

Tourist Offices

The Greek National Tourist Organisation (EOT) maintains offices in:

Australia and New Zealand: 51–57 Pitt Street, Sydney, NSW 2000 (tel: 2411 663)
Canada: 1300 Bay Street, Toronto, Ontario, M5R 3K8 (tel: 9682 220); 1233 rue de la Montagne, Montreal, Quebec, QC H3G 1Z2 (tel: 871 1535)
UK and Republic of Ireland: 4 Conduit Street, London W1R 0DJ (tel: 071-734 5997)

US: 645 Fifth Avenue, Olympic Tower, New York, NY 10022 (tel: 212-421 5777); 611 West Sixth Street, Suite 2198, Los Angeles, California 90017 (tel: 213-626 6696); 168 North Michigan Avenue, National Bank of Greece Building, Chicago, Illinois 6-601 (tel: 312-782 1084)
On Rhodes, the National Tourist Organisation provides useful, free brochures, maps, time-tables and programmes of events. Its main office is found in the centre of Rhodes New Town on Odhos Makariou (tel: 23655, 23255), where the staff will advise on hotels, car rental or sightseeing. The office also stocks a good supply of general information literature. Most of the staff speak English, French or German as well as Greek. The office is open from 07.30 until 15.00hrs. Tourist information desks are also operated by the municipal authorities of Rhodes at the airport, at the port, and in the Old Town. They are open daily from 07.30 until 20.00hrs. Here, too, information is provided in various languages. There is also a tourist information office in Líndhos, located in the main square.

Travel Agencies

There are numerous travel agencies in Rhodes Town and in all the major holiday resorts throughout the island which will arrange accommodation for you, book airline tickets, or organise sightseeing excursions.
Among the most respected is **Rodos Express**, in Papanikolaou and Amerikis streets, Rhodes Town (tel: 21303).

LANGUAGE

Unless you know the Greek script, a vocabulary is not of very much use to the visitor. But it is helpful to know the alphabet, so that you can find your way around, and the following few basic words and phrases will help too.

Alphabet

Alpha	Αα	short a, as in hat
Beta	Ββ	v sound
Gamma	Γγ	guttural g sound
Delta	Δδ	hard th, as in father
Epsilon	Εε	short e
Zita	Ζζ	z sound
Eta	Ηη	long e, as in feet
Theta	Θθ	soft th, as in think
Iota	Ιι	short i, as in hit
Kappa	Κκ	k sound
Lambda	Λλ	l sound
Mu	Μμ	m sound
Nu	Νν	n sound
Xi	Ξξ	x or ks sound
Omicron	Οο	short o, as in pot
Pi	Ππ	p sound
Rho	Ρρ	r sound
Sigma	Σσ	s sound
Taf	Ττ	t sound
Ipsilon	Υυ	another ee sound, or y as in funny
Phi	Φφ	f sound
Chi	Χχ	guttural ch, as in loch
Psi	Ψψ	ps, as in chops
Omega	Ωω	long o, as in bone

Numbers

1	éna	14	dekatéssera
2	dío	15	dekapénde
3	tria	16	dekaéxi
4	téssera	17	dekaeptá
5	pénde	18	dekaoktó
6	éxi	19	dekaennía
7	eptá	20	íkosi
8	októ	30	triánda
9	ennía	40	saránda
10	déka	50	penínda
11	eńdeka	100	ekató
12	dódeka	101	ekaton éna
13	dekatría	1000	chília

In myth the sun god's chariot drives over the horizontal sunset

LANGUAGE

Basic vocabulary

good morning kaliméra
good evening kalispéra
goodnight kaliníkta
goodbye chérete
hello yásou
thank you efcharistó
please/you're welcome parakaló
yes ne
no óchi
where is...? poo íne?
how much is...? póso káni?
I would like tha íthela
do you speak English? milate
  angliká?
I don't speak Greek then miló
  helliniká

Places

street odhos
avenue leofóros
square platía
restaurant estiatório
hotel xenodochío
room domátio
post office tachithromío
letter grámma
stamps grammatóssima
police astinomía
customs teloniakos
passport diavatirion
pharmacy farmakia
doctor iatrós
dentist odontiatros
entrance isothos
exit éxothos
bank trápeza
church eklisía
hospital nosokomío
café kafeneion

Travelling

car aftokíinito
bus leoforio
train tréno
boat karávi
garage garaz

train station stathmos
bus station stasi ton leoforio
airport aerodromio
ticket isitrio

Food and Drink

food fagitó
bread psomi
water neró
wine krasí
beer bira
coffee kafé

Fish

lobster astakós
squid kalamarákia
octopus oktapóthi
red mullet barboúnia
whitebait marídes
sea bream sinagritha

Meat/poultry

lamb arnáki
chicken kotópoulo
meat balls kefthedes
meat on a skewer souvlákia
liver skití

Vegetables

spinach spanáki
courgette kolokithia
beans fasolia

Salads and Starters

olives eliés
yoghurt and cucumber dip tzatziki
tomato and cucumber salad
  angour domata
stuffed vine leaves dolmadakia
'Greek' salad with cheese horiatiki

Desserts

honeycake baklavá
honey puffs loukoumádes
semolina cake halvá
ice-cream pagotó
yoghurt yiaourti
shredded wheat and honey kataifi
custard tart bougatsa